Management Extra

LEADING TEAMS

ELSEVIER

e**LEARN**

Pergamon
Flexible
Learning

AMSTERDAM • BOSTON • HEIDELBERG • LONDON • NEW YORK • OXFORD • PARIS •
SAN DIEGO • SAN FRANCISCO • SINGAPORE • SYDNEY • TOKYO

Pergamon Flexible Learning is an imprint of Elsevier
Linacre House, Jordan Hill, Oxford OX2 8DP, UK
30 Corporate Drive, Suite 400, Burlington, MA 01803, USA

First published 2005
Revised edition 2008

© 2008 Wordwide Learning Limited adapted by Elearn Limited
Published by Elsevier Ltd. All rights reserved.

British Library Cataloguing in Publication Data
A catalogue record for this book is available from the British Library

Library of Congress Cataloging-in-Publication Data
A catalog record for this book is available from the Library of Congress

ISBN 978-0-08-055481-5

For information on all Pergamon Flexible Learning publications visit
our web site at www.elsevierdirect.com

Printed and bound in Hungary

Contents

Activities

Figures

Tables

Series preface

Whether you are a tutor/trainer or studying management development to further your career, Management Extra provides an exciting and flexible resource helping you to achieve your goals. The series is completely new and up-to-date, and has been written to harmonise with the 2004 national occupational standards in management and leadership. It has also been mapped to management qualifications, including the Institute of Leadership & Management's middle and senior management qualifications at Levels 5 and 7 respectively on the revised national framework.

For learners, coping with all the pressures of today's world, Management Extra offers you the flexibility to study at your own pace to fit around your professional and other commitments. Suddenly, you don't need a PC or to attend classes at a specific time – choose when and where to study to suit yourself! And, you will always have the complete workbook as a quick reference just when you need it.

For tutors/trainers, Management Extra provides an invaluable guide to what needs to be covered, and in what depth. It also allows learners who miss occasional sessions to 'catch up' by dipping into the series.

This series provides unrivalled support for all those involved in management development at middle and senior levels.

Reviews of Management Extra

I have utilised the Management Extra series for a number of Institute of Leadership and Management (ILM) Diploma in Management programmes. The series provides course tutors with the flexibility to run programmes in a variety of formats, from fully facilitated, using a choice of the titles as supporting information, to a tutorial based programme, where the complete series is provided for home study. These options also give course participants the flexibility to study in a manner which suits their personal circumstances. The content is interesting, thought provoking and up-to-date, and, as such, I would highly recommend the use of this series to suit a variety of individual and business needs.

Martin Davies BSc(Hons) MEd CEngMIMechE MCIPD FITOL FInstLM
Senior Lecturer, University of Wolverhampton Business School

At last, the complete set of books that make it all so clear and easy to follow for tutor and student. A must for all those taking middle/senior management training seriously.

Michael Crothers, ILM National Manager

The power of teams

Simply stated, a team attitude is a 'we' and 'our' attitude instead of a 'me' and 'my' attitude. When you become part of a team, you're not giving up your individual goals, you're not sacrificing your personal success. You are setting your sights on an even higher goal so that you can magnify your success. Whatever an individual can achieve, a team can do bigger, faster, more effectively, and more gloriously

Source: Pat Williams, former NBA coach, author

Effective teamwork is just as important in the workplace as it is in the world of professional sport. It increases productivity and job satisfaction, with the opposite being true of poor teamworking. It follows, then, that one of the most valuable contributions you can make as a manager is to use your skills and qualities to build a really successful team.

This aim of this book is to help you build, lead and improve teams. You start in the first theme by looking at why teamworking has become such a prevalent force in the global workplace and at the many different types of teams that now exist.

You then move on to leadership. So much about teamwork depends upon the quality of the leader. You explore contemporary thinking on leadership, in particular situational leadership and action-centred leadership, and plan to develop your own leadership skills.

How do you transform a group of individuals into a team? This fundamental question is the focus in our third theme. You apply your leadership skills to the challenge of developing your own team and consider whether it has the right blend of skills for high performance.

In our final theme you look at how you can improve teamworking, with topics on empowerment, decision making in teams and team learning.

Your objectives are to:

◆ Appreciate the pivotal role of teams in the workplace and the characteristics that differentiate high-performing teams

◆ Analyse your leadership style and plan to develop your leadership skills

◆ Explore ways in which you can build a high-performing team

◆ Plan to improve teamworking using the techniques of empowerment, team decision making and team learning.

1   The shape of teams

Teams are made up of individuals – each unique in their values, attitudes, personality, talent, motivation, perception and abilities. An essential role of the team leader is to recognise and harness the talents of each individual and enable them to contribute to their full potential. This is managing individual difference – something you will consider later in this theme.

But a team is more than a group of people who are working together. Katzenbach and Smith define a team as:

> ...a small number of people with complementary skills who are committed to a common purpose, performance goals and approach, for which they hold themselves mutually accountable.

Source: *Katzenbach and Smith* (1994)

In other words, to be a team, the members must pursue a common goal and must agree that the only way to achieve that goal is to *work together*. Success depends on how effectively the individuals are able to collaborate. In a team, this is more important than any one individual's skills. Of course you'll have people who are brighter or more gifted than others, but from your point of view, there is a fine balance between recognising these contributions and ensuring everyone puts their efforts into working for the team.

Teams are not a new concept, but as organisations have flattened out their hierarchies over the past decade the demands on them have altered. New types of teams have emerged that make it possible for an organisation to be more flexible in the way it responds to its environment. These teams pose new challenges for managers, particularly when they need to be put together quickly or when the members are operating virtually.

In this theme you will:

◆ **Recognise the characteristics of a successful team**

◆ **Explore the benefits of diversity and what is meant by managing individual difference**

◆ **Identify how developments in the workplace are transforming team structures**

◆ **Differentiate between types of teams and assess the implications of these team structures for managers.**

Why teamworking?

Work is a complex matter and teamwork can help you handle these complexities.

> An organisation that can't handle complexity is doomed to deliver only the most simple products and services. More sophisticated planning methods might help but there is often no substitute for having the right people involved, together, as a team.

Source: *Chaudhry-Lawton et al.* (1993)

A cohesive team benefits the organisation. However, there are also important benefits for individuals – both the individuals on the team and for you, as the line manager. Table 1.1 highlights what some of these might be.

For the organisation	For the manager	For the team member
Work towards the same goals	All available talent is used	Know what they must achieve
Team objectives are in line with business objectives	Team members are accountable to one another – not just you	Feels supported and respected
		Is encouraged to ask questions
Reduced costs – if job satisfaction levels are higher, there will be lower turnover	Problems are solved as a team	Their opinion is valued
	Can trust the team to get things done	High level of trust. Will try new things and learn from their mistakes
Creativity is enhanced		
Willing and able to adapt to change	Conflict is creative not destructive	
Business objectives can be achieved	Evaluate their own effectiveness willingly	

Table 1.1 *The benefits of teamworking*

The characteristics of a successful team

What makes an effective team?
So what, exactly, is an effective team? An effective team is open to ideas, achieves its goals, has high team commitment, is adaptive to change and is highly rated by upper management. However, whether a team is effective or not comes down to three determining factors:

1 The people within the team – including personal work satisfaction, mutual trust of colleagues and management, low conflict, no power struggles and good job security.

2 The organisation's rules and culture.

3 The tasks to be completed – including objectives, appropriate leadership, challenging work, appropriately skilled team members and team involvement in decisions.

It is easy to understand how organisational rules and job tasks impact on each other, but it is much more difficult to appreciate the impact of people-related factors such as trust.

Trust is a major component that allows people to form good working teams that achieve results. The primary responsibility for creating trust falls on the manager.

Yet data from the USA indicates more than half of staff do not believe what their firm's top management tells them, and over a third do not trust their immediate bosses.

Source: *Harvard Davis (2001)*

The measures given in Table 1.2 are a useful way of assessing your own team. They focus on the importance of relationships within the team, the organisation and the performance of the tasks. Table 1.2 also highlights the importance of balancing individual needs with the needs of the team, which is an idea you'll come across later in this book.

Purpose	Members can describe and are committed to a common purpose
	Goals are clear, challenging and relevant to purpose
	Strategies for achieving goals are clear
	The purpose is aligned to the organisational strategy
Performance	Progress is measurable
	Team rewards are evident
	Specific objectives are set within agreed timescales
	High standards of quality and output
Relationships	Individual roles are clear
	Members are individually accountable
	Members perform different roles and skills as required
	Individual roles are recognised and appreciated
Communication	Members express themselves openly and honestly
	Members listen actively to each other
	Different ideas and approaches are explored
	The team communicates with the wider organisation
Learning	Skills gaps are recognised and training provided
	Members coach each other
	The team reviews its learning on a regular basis
	Team accomplishments are recognised

Table 1.2 *Characteristics of high-performing teams*   Source: *Jones et al. (1996)*

Whether your team is effective by these standards will, to some extent, depend on how long you have worked together. For example, a new team may still act like a group of individuals who you have to manage closely, whereas an experienced team may naturally fall into roles that get the job done.

Clearly, the organisation, the work itself and the individuals on the team will have an impact on how long it takes to become truly effective. But perhaps the single most important factor is you and the strategies you adopt for developing the team to reach its true potential.

Activity 1
Looking at your team

Objective

This activity will help you to consider the purpose and characteristics of teams. It asks you to analyse the opinions and suggestions of members of your own team about how they work together as a team.

Task

At the next team meeting, discuss the following points with team members:

1 The purpose of the team – what it is trying to achieve and why it exists at all.

2 The roles within the team and how those roles contribute to the overall purpose of the team.

3 The benefits of working within a team.

4 Improvements or changes that could be made to the way the team works.

Document the results on flip charts. Then, when consensus has been reached, provide everyone with a definitive and agreed summary giving:

♦ the purpose

♦ how roles contribute to that purpose

♦ the benefits, as identified by the team

♦ any planned improvements, with timescales.

Feedback

Clearly the results will depend on who you talk to, the level of maturity of your team and the tasks in which they are engaged. Equally important is how willing people are to talk openly to you.

In terms of the purpose of the team, positive responses are statements that reflect how the team's role fits in with the overall aims of the organisation. In other words, how they contribute to fulfilling the strategy of the organisation. If this does not come across when you meet with team members, it is something you need to make clear when you deliver the results back to the team.

Similarly, when looking at individual roles and how they fit in with the overall purpose of the team, the best discussions are those that centre on taking a strategic view, rather than listing the key tasks people carry out day to day.

It's very easy for people to concentrate on what they do (input), rather than looking at the results and what they contribute (output). Again, these are important points to reinforce at the team meeting. It is a good way to build individual confidence and help individuals answer the question: 'Why am I here?'

The potential benefits of teamworking are many, such as having the support of others, using everyone's skills and solving problems creatively. If some members of the team struggle to highlight the benefits, you'll need to take action. It is probably worth putting together a list of possible benefits and asking the team to highlight the ones they identify with.

If the team can't identify with many or any of them, you may need to consider making changes to the way the team works – and the way you lead them.

Finally, in terms of ideas for improvement and change, all suggestions should be welcomed and considered seriously. If you receive a lot of suggestions, don't assume that the team is not functioning properly. It means quite the opposite.

If people feel able to put their ideas forward in a constructive way, this demonstrates the team is working well. It means that people are willing to contribute without fear, and that you are leading your team in a way that is perceived as being open and approachable.

Diversity within teams

There is an increasing interest in how organisations can practically embrace and benefit from the diversity within their own workforces.

Legislation in the UK demands that organisations provide equal opportunities for people in the workplace. A focus on diversity and inclusion takes us one step further – its emphasis is on recognising and valuing individual difference in its broadest sense.

In their research for the Institute of Personnel and Development, Fullerton and Kandola (1998) identified the following benefits of managing diversity in organisations:

♦ The organisation employs the best possible candidates

♦ The organisational culture is one in which the potential of all employees is realised

♦ Flexible working arrangements enable the organisation to work more effectively in today's diverse and fast-paced environment

♦ Employees are valued, motivated and encouraged to develop

♦ Employees will have greater job satisfaction and be reluctant to leave

♦ The workforce is likely to reflect a more diverse customer base.

Source: *Adapted from Fullerton and Kandola* (1998)

These benefits have important implications when viewed in the light of trends in the social environment.

Did you know that in the UK:

♦ In 1971 there were 16 million in the labour force and by 2001 this had risen to 16.5 million

♦ In 1971, there were 10 million women in the labour force and by 2001 this had risen to 14.1 million

♦ By 2006, 45–59 year olds will form the largest group in the labour force

♦ In 2003, just over 6 million people in employment were estimated to work flexibly (for example job share and term-time working)

♦ In 2000, a higher proportion of girls (56 per cent) obtained five or more GCSE grade A* to C than boys (46 per cent)

◆ There are over 8 million people with disabilities – almost 15 per cent of the population, of whom 7.1 million are of working age

◆ Less than 8 per cent of people with disabilities are wheelchair users

Source: *Office for National Statistics* (www) *and The Grass Roots Group* (2003)

For employers who are facing skills shortages and trying to retain their talent, being able to manage diversity is now a serious business issue.

The diverse characteristics of individuals

Managing individual difference means helping everyone to reach their full potential and give of their best in achieving the organisation's goals. But what makes up individual difference?

The key variables are shown in Figure 1.1.

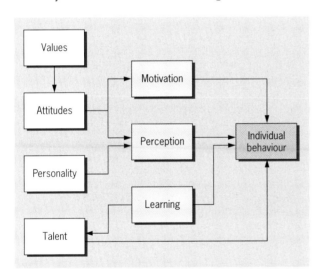

Figure 1.1 *Key variables in individual behaviour*

Source: *Robbins shown in Keuning* (1998)

Everyone has their own values, attitudes, personality, talent, motivation, perception and ability to learn. The nature of these attributes and the way they work together are what make people different.

Values: these are the basic convictions we all have about what is good and what is bad. They are deep-rooted, long-lasting and you'll find they are difficult to change. They affect a person's attitude and behaviours.

Attitudes: these are the positive and negative judgements we make about people and events. They are influenced by basic values and will affect behaviours. While values are unlikely to change, some attitudes can change over time.

Attitudes are not the same as values. Values are wide, more comprising. An attitude is more specific. Human beings have thousands of attitudes, of which the most important for an organisation are: job satisfaction (attitude with regard to the job), involvement (degree of identification with the job), and dedication (degree of loyalty to and identification with the organisation).

Source: *Keuning* (1998)

Personality: Personality is what leads people to behave or act in a particular way. Research and debate about personality have been going on for many years, but clearly it has an influence on work. The key question regarding personality is how much is inherited and how much is learned. This is the nature versus nurture debate.

Four personality attributes

The following four personality attributes are used to define behaviour in more detail: locus of control, authoritarianism, Machiavellianism and risk acceptance.

One can speak of an internal locus of control when people believe they can control their own destiny. People who think that whatever happens is by accident or luck, work from an external locus of control. Employees who are, to a high degree, driven externally, are alienated from their work sooner and are less involved than internally driven people.

One can speak of authoritarianism when someone thinks that status and power differences belong in an organisation. Authoritarian-orientated people are intellectually rigid, are quick in judging others, have respect for higher placed persons, exploit lower placed colleagues, are suspicious and are resistant to change.

Machiavellianism is closely related to authoritarianism. Someone who is strongly Machiavellian-orientated is pragmatic, keeps an emotional distance and believes that the end justifies the means.

People who have high-risk acceptance make decisions more quickly and based on less information than people who tend to take little risk.

The 'theory of personalities' states that the job satisfaction of an employee, and his tendency to change jobs, depends on the degree to which his personality is in harmony with his working environment.

Source: *Keuning* (1998)

Talent: this is to do with the ability and intelligence of the individual. It includes things like verbal and numerical reasoning, mechanical abilities and judgement. Clearly the level of a person's talent will matter in how they perform their job – the level of talent must be in line with the needs of the job. However, other factors are probably even more relevant such as attitude, commitment and motivation.

Motivation: this is the will to do something. It is influenced by the individual's requirement to have certain needs satisfied. You can put pressure on an individual to do something, but this is not true motivation. True motivation comes from within.

Perception: this is the way individuals give meaning to what they see around them. As with other factors of individual difference, people perceive things in very different ways. This leads them to make very different judgements about the world around them.

Ability to learn: this is to do with bringing about a change in behaviour based on experience. It is clear that the better an individual is at learning, the bigger the impact this will have on their talent or ability to do the job.

What does this mean for me?

Knowing something about individual difference can help you understand why people respond in different ways. It can help you appreciate why some people seem to fit in better than others, why people respond to different kinds of reward and why some people respond well to change and others don't.

While it seems impossible to change values, you may be able to change attitudes – although it can be a long and difficult process. Attitude at work is an important factor because it impacts behaviour, which affects motivation and job performance. Therefore if someone has different attitudes from the rest of the team they may find it difficult to fit in. They may feel isolated and under-perform, and you may have to act on this by reinforcing positive attitudes, for example through clear measures. You can then provide rewards for positive changes.

Because everyone views the world in different ways, this has an impact on their way of working. This can lead to conflict or co-operation within your team – a situation that you will have to manage.

The key learning point is that individuals will need to be treated differently if you want to get the best out of the team effort.

The place of work in an individual's life

While the workplace is becoming more diverse and individual difference continues to be important, there's an added complication. The place of work in an individual's life changes over time, depending on how important work is compared with other aspects of their life.

For example:

- wanting to spend more time with children or caring for other family members
- beginning a course of study such as a university degree
- starting a new business venture outside work
- getting involved in community, political or other social groups
- wishing to spend more time on hobbies or interests
- getting over an illness and being told to slow down.

As a manager you are likely to be leading a team with a mixture of priorities – for some their career will be very important, for others it will be less so. It doesn't necessarily mean that some are more committed than others. What it does mean is that you need to understand the role that work plays in their lives. You cannot assume that because some team members work long hours and seem to give 110 per cent that everyone will be – or should be – the same.

Finding out as much as you can about the individuals on your team will help the team to work well together and make your role as leader easier.

Personality

There is a great deal of writing and many theories on personality. If you want to find out more, the work of the following will be of interest:

- Hans Eysenck
- R. Cattell
- Erik Erikson
- Sigmund Freud
- Carl Jung.

One of the major paradoxes of organisational life is the maintenance of individuality and self-responsibility alongside the creation of co-operation and conformity. Managers expect their employees to work with others and be willing to obey; but at the same time expect to see evidence of personality, creativity and independence. Balancing individual needs and goals with group co-operation and conformity can be a major cause of tension, and yet is one of the most important tasks of management.

Source: *Mullins* (1996)

Traditional teams and the need for change

In the past, organisations achieved their objectives by putting people into well-defined roles and telling them exactly what to do. However, the modern workplace demands much greater flexibility. This section explores the backdrop to the changes in teamworking.

The traditional team

You may have experience of a traditional team yourself. In this kind of team everyone had clear tasks, responsibilities and objectives and worked on a daily basis to achieve these. They were seldom required to do anything apart from these key tasks. They were rarely asked for their opinion – and did not dare to offer it. It's quite likely that the manager was an authority figure who made all the decisions. In fact, the members could be described as being part of a work group, rather than a team.

It may have been an efficient way of working – but it could be boring and lacked creativity. Importantly, as job boundaries were so tightly drawn, it allowed little, if any, flexibility.

At the time it didn't really matter. Customers needed the same products and services week in, week out, and they always came back for them. So why was it necessary to change a system that worked?

External forces have brought about enormous changes to organisations' structures and operations. Such changes have had huge implications for individuals and teams who have been forced to adapt in order to meet new customer requirements. The banking sector, for example, has experienced mergers and takeovers, intensifying competition, changing technology such as the Internet, and demands for improved service from customers. In order to survive banks have had to change their structure, their operations and the way individuals and teams work.

Consider what external factors have brought about such massive changes in the way businesses and teams have been transformed.

The need for change

> **If the rate of change on the outside exceeds the rate of change on the inside, the end is near.**
>
> **Jack Welch,** Former Chairman and CEO, General Electric Corp.

The major forces for change come from outside your organisation. These, in turn, require changes to be made internally. Those businesses that cope best are the ones that anticipate change and react quickly. From your point of view, as a manager, you must respond to the opportunities and threats that come from outside, which means facing challenges and risks on a daily basis.

These external factors that bring about the need for change are known as PESTLE factors. These are:

Political

Economic

Social

Technological

Legislative

Eco-environmental

It is these external pressures that can mean you and your team are in a constant state of change, which at times may feel like chaos. Of course if your external environment is fairly static, your team and their way of working may not need to be flexible. On the other hand, if your environment is dynamic, you probably feel the pressures most of the time. However, whether your market is local, national or international these environmental factors will affect you one way or another.

But what sort of factors come under the PESTLE heading? These are outlined here, along with some of the key issues from a UK perspective.

The PESTLE factors

Political: National government action is clearly an important factor here, so is any action taken by the European Union that affects member states. Indeed the common European currency is having a major impact on business across the EU.

Economic: Few organisations have totally escaped the move towards globalisation. The movement of labour-intensive jobs, such as in manufacturing, to developing countries has had a severe impact on jobs in the developed world. This threat still hangs over many businesses today, forcing a radical rethink and restructuring. Nationally, tax and interest rates affect business, for example by increasing or decreasing consumer spending.

Social: This includes factors such as the ageing population and lower birth rates, which mean that there are less young people available for work. Families are also changing, with more one-parent families and more parents at work. Where good employees are hard to find, organisations must look at how to retain the skills they have. Business may have to pay more – but it's just as likely these people will look for other benefits such as flexible working.

Technological: Of all the factors, this has had the greatest impact in recent years in the UK and most of the developed world. It has helped to simplify some jobs, while others have disappeared completely. Communication is faster than ever before, and while the dot-com bubble may have burst, technology will continue to impact on everyone's working life.

> Within a computerised working situation...traditional dividing lines between occupational categories break down and the demarcation of jobs can become irrelevant; vertically as well as horizontally. There is much more scope for job rotation, undermining thereby employees' specific control over what were previously highly specialised jobs that could not easily be given to other categories of worker.

Source: *Bennett* (1997)

Legislative: New laws in areas such as health and safety, and employee welfare also force change. In addition, a new government is likely to bring in new legislation, which can help or hinder your progress. Again, in Europe, EU legislation is likely to have as big an impact as national legislation, for example the changes to reduce working hours and the introduction of paternity leave for new fathers.

Eco-environmental: Ecological issues have become an increasing concern for many in recent years at both individual and organisational level. This is particularly the case for global multi-nationals, which are constantly in the public eye. However discussions on factors such as global warming are resolved, it is likely that firms will be restricted in future to minimise their environmental impact – certainly in Europe, if not the USA.

Political	Closer alliance with EU – ability to recruit sales people in Europe
	Local government changes – possible increase in local business rates
Economic	Strength of the currency – impact cost per sale (needsmarter ways of doing business)
	Increased tax on petrol – less travel a requirement
Social	Lifestyle balance – some of the team request home-based working (carer responsibility)
Technological	Technology obsolete – new laptops needed to keep up-to-date.
	Phone enhancements – allow salespeople to work effectively in remote locations.
	E-learning – no need to bring together for training
Legislative	Work time directive – the need to look for ways to restrict hours of working
	Health & safety laws in pipeline – change to work practice?
Eco-environmental	Emissions regulations – the impact on running company cars
	Ability to source raw materials from developing world

Table 1.3 *How PESTLE factors affect a sales team in a UK engineering company*

Table 1.3 shows you the impact of these PESTLE factors on a sales team in a small engineering firm in the UK.

How PESTLE affects your team

How the PESTLE factors affect your team will obviously depend on where you work. In the majority of cases, it is technology that has had the biggest impact. For example, thanks to technology, there is no need for a team to physically work together. People can work from home, on the train, and even from abroad. It has also enabled global organisations to put teams together on a worldwide basis. They can draw on expertise around the globe to put a team together for a specific project – and you may have to manage them.

On the social side, the demand for flexible working may mean that it is rare for your team to all be together in one place – some may work term-time only, some may be home-based, some may work annualised hours. Again this brings new pressures on you as their manager to co-ordinate work, maintain motivation and communicate with everyone.

In addition, political and economic factors may force changes in the way the team is structured. For example, new government family-friendly policies may mean you have to cover staff absence that you hadn't anticipated. Economic changes may mean that there is a sudden demand to get a new product or service to market urgently.

While you as an individual manager can do nothing to influence these PESTLE factors, what you can do is keep abreast of these changes. If you can anticipate what some of these changes might be, then you can plan how you and your team can best adapt to them and carry on working as an efficient unit. Having an awareness of PESTLE factors helps you plan how to structure your team to make the most of opportunities and counter any threats.

The key is to remain competitive in the face of a rapidly changing external environment. For example, the response to the slump in the 1980s was downsizing, which meant tiers of managers losing their jobs while those who remained had a greater span of control, which brought its own challenges. Another response might be to introduce technology in an attempt to develop new products and bring these to market ahead of the competition. Alternatively, managers might seek out new markets for the same products.

There will often be a range of responses available to you – the skill is choosing the right one and implementing it in a timely manner.

New approaches to teamworking

Different types of teams have emerged over the years, in line with the changing needs of organisations. Businesses themselves have become more flexible and your organisation is likely to have a flatter structure than it did, maybe five or ten years ago. Layers of bureaucracy may have been stripped away, leaving you with fewer managers who must organise their teams in response to this.

The point is that new types of teams function best in a non-bureaucratic organisation, where team processes have been established, so that any new team has a solid foundation to build on. A new team can become more effective more quickly if the team processes are in place to support it. This also means that the organisation must value people behaviours that support fast team formation.

So what are these new types of teams? The main ones are outlined here.

Cross-functional teams

Cross-functional teams are put together across departments and functions to achieve a particular objective. They may work on this basis full or part-time until the objective is achieved. The team is made up of people with the necessary skills and expertise, usually in quite specific areas, which they can then contribute to the team effort. Cross-functional teams are usually assembled to meet the need of a major organisational initiative such as new product development, a change or business improvement programme.

If you are in charge of a cross-functional team, you have the advantage of managing the best in the business to get the job done. On the other hand, people may only see the issues from their own perspective, which can be a major challenge for you.

Self-managed teams

A true self-managed team is a leaderless team, in that there is no one in a senior position in charge. What can happen is the leadership role is rotated so the team can maintain direction and focus. Self-managed teams, in the true sense of the word, have not become as widespread as anticipated. This is partly because it's sometimes difficult to function in this way. Also because the team takes on all the work that is usually performed by a manager, such as budgeting, project management, work allocation and problem solving. This often requires a good deal of training or a natural leader emerges who has these skills already.

Self-managed teams at Vesuvius in Ayrshire

This former lace-making plant was taken over by Vesuvius of Pittsburgh in the 1960s. It now makes ceramics and other components for the steel industry. With a head office in Brussels and no local markets or raw supplies, it decided there was a need for change.

In 1994 it embarked on a change programme under the banner of the business excellence model developed by the European Foundation for Quality Management (EFQM). Designed to create a culture in which all employees took responsibility for improved performance, this programme centred on the introduction of self-managed teams.

For the teams to succeed, new working practices were needed. Over successive wage negotiations from 1994 to 1997, the various rates traditionally paid for different production jobs were replaced with a single wage structure and complete labour flexibility across jobs and departments. Production workers were given training that enabled every member of every team to do all the jobs within that team. For a workforce where the average length of service was 15 years, the idea of teams taking responsibility – for the tasks that they carried out, the materials that they used and the problems that they encountered – represented a complete break from the way they had worked in the past.

The foremen were also required to apply their minds to an extensive development programme designed to equip them for their new role as facilitators. Training in fact, has become a way of life at the Newmilns plant where all 185 workers have now reached at least NVQ level 1.

But the ultimate measure of success comes from the company's results. Vesuvius Scotland's turnover rose from £37 million in 1993 to £55 million in 1998 – an increase the company attributes to the competitive edge gained from empowering its employees and giving them responsibility for quality.

Source: *Arkin* (1999)

To find out about the model developed by the European Foundation for Quality Management, see www.efqm.org

Virtual teams

As the name suggests, these are teams put together on a national or international basis, relying on the latest technology for their communication. Apart from at the beginning of a project, they may seldom meet, so must keep in contact through phone, e-mail and video-conferencing. As with the cross-functional team, they are put together for particular projects, rather than working together on a regular basis. They can be expensive to set up, support and maintain, but are often necessary when an organisation needs diverse experience and expertise.

Global teams

Global teams are increasingly used by large organisations to pool talent. This is often to develop a strategy for penetrating new markets, where global representatives can talk about the needs of customers in their particular region. As with virtual teams, this can be a costly business. The technology must be in place, a new approach to teamwork is required, and since people are working with a number of different nationalities they require training in diversity and cultural awareness.

An underlying cause of the success or lack thereof of global teams may reside in the definition of what it takes to be a good team member or leader. Cultural values play a significant role in those definitions. For example, a French team member may jump in to assist a US colleague he or she perceives is in need of help. Americans, however, have a strong desire to act as individuals; thus, the US team member may interpret the French colleague as undermining his or her job by interfering.

Source: *Bing and Mercer Bing* (2001)

Quality teams

As the name suggests, these are groups of people who meet regularly to analyse and solve problems relating to quality within the organisation, in areas such as production and working practices. The problems they solve are usually organisation-wide, taking the team members beyond the remit of their usual roles. Membership of the group is voluntary and the issues discussed are identified by the team itself. The outcome is generally recommended solutions that are then put to management. They are similar in many ways to improvement teams, which look at improvements across the organisation, beyond the remit of quality.

Customer–supplier teams

These teams consist of representatives from the organisation and either customers or suppliers. They look at various aspects of the supply chain and customer service, as a way of making improvements. They are generally formed with long-term, important customers and suppliers where improving ways of working are critical to the relationship.

The challenges for management

If you are put in charge of any of these teams you will face very different challenges from those you are used to. With cross-functional and self-managed teams you have the advantage of being able to meet everyone face to face. With virtual and global teams this is not the case.

Managing teams remotely means you will probably need a whole new skill set and may feel your role is one of administrator. You are dealing with people who may be working in different time zones, therefore communication structures, such as using your intranet and e-mail, must be very tight. Similarly, scheduling will require careful consideration, especially as yours may be only one of a number of projects – and may be quite low priority at that. Progress reports are essential and, as with all other communication, they should be fed into the system for comment and feedback. You may have to get used to a whole new set of business practices – or others will have to adapt to yours.

Your role in managing cross-functional and self-managed teams will be quite different. In a traditional team you are probably in a senior position and able to control and direct resources. In a cross-functional team there may be people at different levels of seniority. However, someone still needs to provide a leadership role and to co-ordinate all players and ensure communication is clear and thorough. So the leadership role becomes one of a facilitator for both self-managed and cross-functional teams.

In all cases, there may be some problem matching the people to the work – if you don't know them well. This will particularly be the case if using subcontractors. Once the team is established, people must be very clear about what outcomes you want – and how you will measure effectiveness, both on a team and individual basis.

Activity 2
Team structures

Objective

This activity will help you to assess the way team structures affect performance and how improvements can be made.

Task

Make notes on a team that you currently work with to assess what impact its structure has on its performance. This may be the team you manage on a day-to-day basis, but it can also be another team you lead. It might include project teams, cross-functional teams, global or virtual teams.

Use the following questions as a way of guiding your thinking.

1   *Do the members feel part of a team?*

2   *Do the team members have a clear purpose and defined objectives, and is everyone clear about these?*

3   *Does everyone on the team identify with everyone else on the team?*

4   *Do they need to, and are they willing to, help one another to achieve their objectives?*

5   *Is there more co-operation than conflict?*

6   *Is any conflict that arises seen as constructive and does it help the team to be creative?*

7   *Do you find it easy to communicate with all members of the team?*

8   *Do team members communicate with one another in the most effective way possible?*

9   Does the team communicate and co-operate with other teams when required?

10   Do you find it easy to co-ordinate the work of all the team members?

11   Do systems and procedures support the team in what it is trying to achieve?

12   Are members of the team able and willing to make decisions without deferring to you all the time?

13   Does the present structure provide opportunities for individual development?

In light of the above, what improvements would you make, if any, to the present team structure?

Feedback

You will have noticed that the numbered questions are all framed in a positive way. In other words, if you can answer 'yes' to them all, you have a healthy team that is probably working within the correct team structure.

If you have considered your own team for this activity, and it is a relatively stable team, your results are probably more positive than if, for instance, you have looked at a new cross-functional or global team.

This does not necessarily mean the structure of such teams is wrong – in fact, it may be the only team structure that is feasible. What it can mean is that the challenges for you, as the leader of such a team, are different.

You'll probably have to take more time to build the team, so that members feel that they're part of it, as well as making the team into something with which they clearly identify. Objectives will need to be reinforced – perhaps several times. Establishing a clear direction, which is understood by everyone, gives a team purpose and identity. It helps everyone channel their personal efforts and energies in the same direction.

If you don't take time to put these things in place, people will not feel part of the team. You may find that rather than working together, members tend to work against one another. Small sub-groups form around particular areas of self-interest, and members of these groups put all their energy into undermining the team for their own ends. For example, they do not co-operate with other team members and fail to communicate – even keeping key information to themselves.

These new team structures also need different systems and procedures. These need to be in place at an early stage and the responsibility for ensuring that this is the case rests with you. If you are working with remote teams, the communication system, in particular, is fundamental to the success of the team.

In addition, while the needs of the team and its task are important, the needs of the individual should not be neglected. People still need development opportunities and, as a manager, you will always need to pay attention to these needs.

Therefore, before considering a change to the way the team is structured, make sure the team is given every opportunity to work effectively. By ensuring that the factors thrown up by the questions in this activity are dealt with effectively, you are giving your team the best opportunity to succeed.

Activity 3
New trends in teamworking

Objective

Use this activity to review the challenges that face managers and staff working with global teams.

While the development of technology is making the use of global teams more common, you need to think carefully about the challenges this type of teamworking brings.

Case study

Read the following case study.

21

Future hinges on global teams

The new four cylinder engines that will power Saturn LS sedans off a Delaware assembly line next year will be more than just another job-well-done for Rita Forst, one of hundreds worldwide who could be a poster child for the 21st century auto industry.

For her and dozens more General Motors Corp. engineers and executives, the debut of the new engine will be proof that it's possible to work globally in a world still defined by different languages, cultures and national borders.

'It's very easy to ... create a team on a piece of paper,' says Forst, 43, an engine integration manager for the 2.2-litre engine, code-named L-850. 'But to create a global organisation, you really have to move people around. Out of that come personal relationships. A team has to live.'

As GM, Ford Motor Co., Daimler Chrysler AG, Toyota Motor Corp. and Volkswagen AG – the so called 'Global Five' – push to open new markets worldwide, the ability of each company to effectively manage, communicate and move its employees across borders and time zones is likely to make a difference.

If the past is any predictor of the future, Americans will be pushed to understand that the new engines they're developing need to meet rigorous German standards. Germans will be urged to acknowledge, finally, that armrests are nice and cup holders necessary. And the Japanese will be lobbied to make room in their full-size pickups for cowboy hats and American-sized building products.

The challenges are similar, but each of the leading automakers is forging its own road to achieve the holy grail: an integrated global company that uses common parts and manufacturing processes to offer the world's widest range of cars and trucks for the lowest cost and fattest profits.

Source: *Howes* (1998)

Task

Now answer the following questions about working with global teams.

1 According to the case study, what are the major challenges facing organisations working with global teams?

List your answers here:

2   What do you regard as the main advantages and disadvantages of
    working with global teams?

Advantages:

Disadvantages:

3   Using the information in the case study, as well as your own
    understanding, what would you say are the requirements for
    effective global teams?

List the key requirements here:

Feedback

1   According to the case study, the major challenges include
    getting people to overcome barriers of language, culture and
    national borders. The challenge is one of understanding –
    getting people to work as a living team. In addition, the need
    to manage people and communicate with them is of
    paramount importance. The way GM has met these
    challenges is to physically move people around to meet other
    people within their global team. This is an expensive but
    clearly worthwhile option.

2   In terms of advantages, an organisation can draw on talent
    globally and improve its own creativity. It avoids the problem
    of one culture imposing its own stereotypical view on the
    development of products and services for a global market, for
    example, Germans not understanding American consumers'
    desire for cup holders! Disadvantages are likely to include the
    increased complexity of managing different people in
    different countries working towards the same objective. There
    can be a lack of cohesion and understanding, especially in the

early days, and confusion in group processes. There is also the danger that the group may become fragmented, as with any team, but because it is global, creating and maintaining cohesion is particularly difficult.

3 Face-to-face contact from the very start seems to be a key requirement for building an effective global team. It also requires clear objectives and common, clearly understood processes to implement these objectives. Open communication is vital, as is an understanding of cultural differences. It also requires commitment from the leader of the team to help build trust across the team, as well as clear roles and responsibilities. The team also needs to develop shared norms, values and even language.

◆ Recap

Recognise the characteristics of a successful team

◆ Katzenbach and Smith (1994) define a team as 'a small number of people with complementary skills who are committed to a common purpose, performance goals and approach, for which they hold themselves mutually accountable'.

◆ Jones et al. (1996) identify purpose, performance, relationships, communication and learning as the attributes that differentiate a high-performing team.

Explore the benefits of diversity and what is meant by managing individual difference

◆ Globalisation, an ageing population and an increase in flexible working are all factors leading to greater diversity in the workforce. Managing diversity is now a serious business issue for employers.

◆ Diversity means individual difference. Robbins (in Keuning, 1998) identifies seven factors that make people different: values, attitudes, personality, talent, motivation, perception and ability to learn.

◆ To value diversity, we need first to question whether we have preconceived views that lead us to discriminate between people, and then to deepen our understanding of the people we manage so that we can support them to achieve their full potential.

Identify how developments in the workplace are transforming team structures

♦ The word 'team' is used to describe a range of radically different working arrangements. New team structures have emerged in response to the changing business environment, specifically:

  – the demand for more flexible forms of working

  – advances in technology, which enable organisations to select teams on the basis of expertise rather than physical location

  – delayered organisations that can respond more rapidly and flexibly to customer demands, which has implications for old hierarchical team structures.

Differentiate between types of teams and assess the implications of these team structures for managers

♦ Examples of new team structures include cross-functional, self-managed, virtual, global, quality and customer–supplier teams.

♦ There are implications for the team leader who is no longer necessarily the most senior person on the team. A different set of skills that support a more facilitative management style is required.

 **More @**

Katzenbach, J., and Smith, D. (1999) *The Wisdom of Teams: Creating the High-performance Organisation*, McGraw-Hill
Including stories and case examples drawn from interviews with people in over 50 teams, this text seeks to demonstrate why teams will be the primary building blocks of company performance in the 21st century.

Trompenaars, F. and Hampden Turner, C. (1997) *Riding the Waves of Culture: Understanding Cultural Diversity in Business*, Nicholas Brealey Publishing
This book is for managers who want to develop a better understanding of cultural diversity.

Search the websites of the **Chartered Institute of Personnel and Development** (www.cipd.co.uk) and the **Equal Opportunities Commission** (www.eoc.org.uk) for more on diversity and equality of opportunity.

2 | Approaches to leadership

Leadership is said to be a critical determinant of team and organisational effectiveness, but ask the question, 'What is leadership?' and you'll be swamped with definitions. Here are just a few:

> A dynamic process through which influence is exercised over others to commit enthusiastically to the achievement of the group task.

Source: *Wild* (1994)

> Leadership might be interpreted in simple terms, such as 'getting others to follow' or 'getting people to do things willingly'... but essentially it is a relationship through which one person influences the behaviour of other people.

Source: *Mullins* (1996)

> Leadership is the art of getting someone else to do something you want done because he wants to do it.

Source: *Dwight D. Eisenhower, former US President*

> Leadership involves focusing the efforts of a group of people towards a common goal and enabling them to work together as a team.

Source: *Adair* (1987)

> Leadership is the process of motivating other people to act in particular ways in order to achieve specific goals.

Source: *Hannagan* (1998)

This theme explores contemporary thinking on leadership. You will:

◆ Determine why leadership is a requirement of modern management

◆ Review contemporary developments in the field of leadership

◆ Understand why effective leaders adapt their style to fit the situational context

◆ Explore the three areas of need within a team.

The need for leadership

Management used to mean control. However, with the need for flexibility and fewer layers of management in many organisations, there is a greater need for leadership. This means you no longer get people to *comply* with what you want, you must get them to *commit* to what the organisation is trying to achieve.

The traditional manager would probably manage a small team of people who were working towards inflexible team goals. This involved fulfilling their job role as outlined in their job description. The organisation would be structured as a hierarchy and everyone knew where they fitted in – and the tasks they had to do to get the job done. People focused on their own tasks and little else.

Things have changed. Most organisations are now flatter and today you may be in charge of a large team of people with expertise that you haven't got yourself. You might also be working with a number of types of team, such as project teams or virtual teams. The old high levels of control and direction in management are no longer possible – or desirable.

These changes put a very different set of demands on you.

> Today's successful business leaders will be those who are most flexible of mind. An ability to embrace new ideas, routinely challenge old ones, and live with paradox will be the effective leader's premier trait. Further the challenge is for a lifetime. New truths will not emerge easily.

Source: *Peters* (1987)

Management versus leadership

Management is based on position. In other words, you get people to do what you want based on the authority of your job title. You then plan, direct, control, monitor and measure people to make sure they are complying with standards and targets for the job. Traditionally this is a role of command and control. It is task-driven as opposed to outcome-driven.

Leadership, on the other hand, is not necessarily based on position, although it is recognised that the modern manager does require leadership qualities. Leaders are more concerned with the end result – as opposed to the steps taken to achieve that end result. In other words they are outcome-driven, rather than task-driven.

> ...leaders are not commanders and controllers, bosses and big shots. Instead they are servers and supporters, partners and providers.

Source: *Jones et al.* (1996)

Leadership means recognising that there may be different ways to achieve the desired outcome. Therefore you are willing to let the team decide the best ways of doing things for themselves. This doesn't mean you abandon all responsibility for what goes on. On the contrary, you must still plan, make decisions, take risks and be accountable.

In addition to these roles you will also:

◆ engender enthusiasm and creativity

◆ communicate readily – downwards, upwards and across

◆ motivate others and build morale

◆ involve others in decision making

◆ show an interest in people and listen to what they say

◆ allow mistakes to happen – to improve learning

◆ be a good student as well as a teacher

◆ coach and support team members when needed.

In fact, it is a more demanding role than ever before: while you have less control over the methods people use to achieve the outcome, you are still accountable for the end result.

Part of the increase in demand is to do with the unwritten understanding of the work relationship between you, the organisation and the employee. This is known as the psychological contract and it has changed a great deal in recent years.

Leadership and the psychological contract

The idea of the psychological contract relates to the unwritten parts of the employment relationship. It concerns assumptions about what either side is willing to offer. In other words, what the employee is willing to give in return for what the employer will provide.

It is not about the content of what people do, such as their job description or salary, it is about things that are never stated but are assumed, such as feelings of job security and the level of added value an employee will bring in return.

The difficulty for you is that the psychological contract is always changing. For example, reorganisation and redundancy are now part of working life. On the other hand, employers are expecting more in terms of added value. So jobs are no longer secure but the employer expects greater added value than ever before. In other words, the psychological contract is not balanced in the way it was.

The result is that employees tend to be less loyal because they see no loyalty given in return, as the concept of a job for life has all but disappeared. Instead, the individual is looking to make him or herself more employable, leading to greater choice in times when they feel threatened. Therefore, what good employers offer instead is the chance for employability, such as a wider opportunity for development and learning.

Old loyalties are breaking down.

> ...the differences between the generations may be summed up in two words: loyalty versus commitment. The organisation man values loyalty to the company; his children value commitment to a profession. For the organisation man it's 'my company, right or wrong'. For his children it's 'my company right for me or I'm gone.'

Source: *Jones et al.* (1996)

The implications for you

The breakdown in loyalty to the company and growth in loyalty to self has important implications for you, as a manager. If people no longer feel as committed to the organisation, how can you make good people stay?

Part of the answer is to act as leader – rather than manager. Employees are becoming more self-reliant so to make them stay with you, you'll need to build more of a partnership of equals – rather than basing the relationship on your role as manager and them as subordinate.

Basically this means applying all those leadership functions outlined earlier, such as motivation, involvement and communication.

Of course, some people find this easier than others as they have a natural tendency to be leaders. A lot of this is to do with the assumptions you make about how to get the best from your team.

Leadership in three dimensions
I have always regarded management as leadership in three dimensions; economic, entrepreneurial and social.

The economic dimension is instantly recognisable: it includes the professional process of combining commerce, administration and technical skills, towards profitable objectives. A leader has to know the basics of his or her craft. The entrepreneurial side is much more difficult to measure, but what is measurable in management is seldom all there to measure, and is not always the most important. There is an area of imagination and energy, of risk-taking and of risk-making, of seizing the changes that others do not seize, of seeing ahead and somehow shaping the future.

In the social dimension, managers and organisations are far less assured. The role of business managers in co-ordinating the culture of their enterprise and that of the community is rapidly emerging. The trouble is that these two forces do not necessarily thrust in the same direction.

A manager's success in fusing all three dimensions depends on his or her capability to lead. The truth is that people prefer being led to being managed. The process of good leadership makes a leader realise how much depends on others. The leader has to listen to a myriad of different viewpoints, opinions, aspirations and grievances. To do so, leaders have to be accessible – not on an occasional basis, but continually they have to 'be there'.

Source: *Sir Peter Parker quoted by Crainer* (1996)

Activity 4
What you think of people at work

Objective

This activity will help you to determine your underlying attitude towards individuals at work. All managers make assumptions about people on their team. It is useful to analyse those assumptions to see whether they are likely to have a positive or negative impact on your own leadership behaviour.

Task

The pairs of statements in the chart opposite are contrasting opinions about people's attitude to work. Look at each pair and circle the number on the scale that reflects your own views. If you circle 1, you fully agree with the statement in the Theory X column; if you circle 5, you agree completely with the statement in the Theory Y column.

Theory X		Rating	Theory Y
A	People dislike work and will avoid it if possible	1 2 3 4 5	People enjoy work and achievement
B	People must be directed and threatened to make them work hard	1 2 3 4 5	People want to do well and achieve their objectives
C	People are happier with a quiet life and avoid responsibility	1 2 3 4 5	Under proper conditions, most people learn to accept responsibility
D	People are self-centred and indifferent to business needs	1 2 3 4 5	People feel rewarded if they help the business develop
E	People are resistant to change – they don't like making decisions	1 2 3 4 5	People have the creativity to solve the organisation's problems and work with change
F	People are gullible and not particularly bright	1 2 3 4 5	In work, the potential of people is only partly used

Source: *McGregor* (1987)

Now plot your score on the scale below.

Theory X						Theory Y
0	5	10	15	20	25	30

Feedback

This activity is based on the work of Douglas McGregor. He looked at the manager's assumptions about motivation and commitment.

Theory X managers assume employees dislike work, that they don't like responsibility and lack ambition. Therefore, staff must be tightly controlled and directed in what they do.

Theory Y managers believe people enjoy work and will manage their own workloads, co-operating willingly to achieve objectives. They believe people know what they have to do. The manager therefore encourages self-responsibility, as people are already motivated.

You probably found your score was somewhere in the middle. What McGregor found was that managers who scored towards the Y end of the scale got better results and fewer staff problems than those who scored towards the X end of the scale. In other words, these were the managers who displayed leadership skills in addition to the usual roles of management.

The origins of modern leadership

There are many theories on leadership and while no one theory is dominant, you'll find that some are definitely more popular than others. In this section, you explore how leadership thinking has developed in the last 50 years.

Trait approach

This is based on the idea that there are natural leaders, that is, that they are born, not made. The emphasis, therefore, is on identifying the qualities of good leaders.

Research has highlighted factors such as intelligence, initiative and self-assurance as being important – but nobody has been able to agree what the desirable qualities might be.

The other problem with this approach is that it tends to discourage the idea that people can be developed to be leaders, which is clearly not the view today.

One of the most famous writers on trait theories is Edwin Ghiselli whose work became widely known in the early 1970s.

The behavioural approach

This emphasises behaviours rather than qualities, which implies that leadership can be learned. People working in this field looked at what good leaders did in areas such as communication, motivation and decision making. This meant these skills could then be taught.

In his book *Handbook of Leadership* (1974), Ralph Stogdill concluded there were two main themes to leadership – concern for people and concern for the task. He found that employees were happier under managers who were more concerned with people. Research also showed they were less concerned with the actual style and more with the situation under which the style was used.

The management grid

This work was taken a stage further by Blake and Mouton (1985), who developed the management grid. The grid identified 81 different management approaches based on the way task and employee-based styles could react with one another.

At one extreme is the country club manager where concern for people is high and concern for the task is low. The manager here will work to secure the co-operation of staff on a voluntary basis.

Staff are generally happy with this style although the leader can be seen as too lenient and poor at making decisions.

At the other extreme is the authoritarian manager where concern for task is high and concern for people is low. They tend to alienate themselves from the team and, as with any authoritarian approach, the manager makes all the decisions. This results in low team satisfaction.

Contingency approach

This focuses on the situational factors that influence leadership. Tannenbaum and Schmit were among the first to look at this in the 1970s.

They concluded there were three main forces within any situation:

1 Personal forces – the manager him or herself.

2 Subordinates – their willingness or unwillingness to take responsibility.

3 The situation – the tasks to be performed.

They then combined these forces on a continuum.

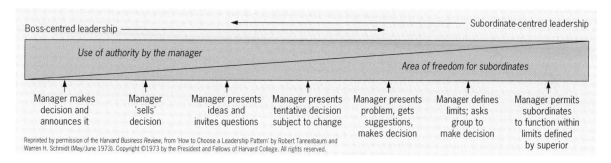

Figure 2.1 *Continuum of leadership behaviour*

Source: *Tannenbaum and Schmit* (1973)

This suggests that you have a full range of options open to you when it comes to deciding what style to use – from the very autocratic to the laissez-faire.

Transactional leadership

The foundation of this theory is that a manager/subordinate relationship is built on exchange. In return for compliance from the employee, the manager provides some form of reward, such as financial recognition or favourite work.

However, it depends on tight organisational structures and clear goals and measures to be effective. It also needs a fairly static work environment to ensure the manager has the power and authority to make the exchange.

Transformational leadership

Transformational leadership, on the other hand, is to do with winning the hearts and minds of employees. The idea is to motivate people to strive for long-term goals, rather than short-term interests. The leader must create trust and commitment, empowering and enabling people to perform.

Transformational leaders are seen as having charisma in their relationship with the group. It relies on being able to influence and persuade, based on a common understanding and shared interest of the team as a whole – including the leader.

The difficulty with this is that it's almost going back to the leaders-are-born-not-made argument. In other words, can charisma be learned or are you born with it?

Leadership styles
The most familiar descriptions of leadership style are autocratic, participative and laissez-faire.

Autocratic leaders rely on the power behind their position. Status is important and they will take control when it comes to things like decision making and providing instruction. They will not ask people's opinions or look for consensus. They respect loyalty from subordinates and discourage participation, criticism or creativity among people. Interpersonal skills are not their strong point.

Participative leaders, on the other hand, have strong interpersonal skills, communicate well with the team and encourage participation. They are likely to seek agreement in decision making. However, they will take difficult decisions if agreement can't be reached. Striving for consensus and creativity are both important features of this style.

As the name suggests, **laissez-faire leaders** will let people get on with things. They will let the team define the problem and seek solutions because they can see the team is working well on its own. The leader allows power to shift to the team and does not interfere. However, the leader is there if support is required.

Activity 5
The way you lead

Objective

Use this activity to examine how effective and efficient you are as a team leader.

Task

The following checklist gives you a starting point to examine your contribution as team leader. It looks at two of the basic requirements of this role. Firstly, you need to be effective – in other words, to achieve what you're supposed to achieve for the organisation. Secondly, you need to be efficient, that is, you have to make the most of all the resources at your disposal.

Tick the relevant boxes where you can honestly answer 'yes' to the question.

Indicators of an effective leader

I have a clear understanding of the organisation's purpose or mission	☐
I know how the organisation's objectives fit in with my department's objectives	☐
I know how my role contributes to what the organisation is trying to achieve	☐
Each member knows where they fit within the team	☐
Individual objectives reflect what we are trying to achieve as a team	☐
Individuals on the team know what outcomes are expected of them	☐
Daily tasks and activities are largely geared towards achieving our objectives	☐
Responsibilities are clearly defined, although people are willing to work flexibly	☐
People are willing to ask questions if we seem to be moving in the wrong direction	☐
People understand where we stand in relation to our main competitors	☐

Indicators of an efficient leader

People have work plans that reflect their objectives	☐
These plans are updated regularly or when the organisation's priorities change	☐
I regularly meet with people on the team to discuss their work performance	☐
My own manager is kept up to date with what we are doing	☐
There is no uncertainty about who is responsible for what	☐
The demands on the team are realistic and achievable	☐
Everyone is responsible for monitoring and managing our resources	☐
Individuals suggest new ways of working that will improve our efficiency	☐
People on my team are willing to try new things	☐
People recognise that teamworking is the right way of doing things	☐

35

Feedback

Being effective and efficient are two basic requirements of leadership – whatever your preferred leadership style. Effectiveness is to do with your own contribution to organisational goals and how you communicate this to your team. Efficiency is how you carry out work activities in the most appropriate way.

The combined result of being effective and efficient means that the activities that you and the team are involved in on a daily basis contribute to what the organisation is aiming to achieve.

If you were able to tick all the statements on the list, it means that you have a solid foundation on which to build your own leadership of the team. If there are a few statements you didn't tick, then look at these again in more detail. Develop an action plan of what you will do to make yourself stronger in these particular areas.

The adaptable leader

One of the most frequently quoted and most extensively used models of leadership is called situational leadership.

What is situational leadership?

Situational leadership depends on both the leader and the team being willing to adapt.

Hersey developed this approach to management in the 1980s. It is based on the idea that the style the manager should adopt is based on the circumstances or situation, but more particularly on the readiness of the team. This means their maturity in terms of their desire for achievement and their willingness to act, that is, to take responsibility for things like making decisions.

Readiness can be divided into four levels:

R1 – In this case the team has low follower readiness. This means that the subordinates are both unable and unwilling to complete the task/fulfil the objective because they lack commitment and motivation. On the other hand, they may be unable and insecure – probably because they are a very new team.

In either case you will need to adopt the style of 'telling'. This means being directive in the way people should complete the task. So you will give detailed instructions and monitor carefully. You are less concerned with the relationship building at this stage so may show low relationship behaviour.

R2 – This is a team with low to moderate follower readiness. They may be unable and willing or they may be unable and confident. In either case they are motivated but still lack the ability – even if the confident ones don't realise it yet.

Here the style is referred to as 'selling'. You will still need to direct the task carefully, but by this stage you are showing high relationship behaviour. It means, for example, giving more explanation of why you're asking people to do this task and allowing them to ask questions.

R3 – This refers to a team that has moderate to high follower readiness. They may be able to complete the task but feel insecure about doing so. Or they may be able to perform but are unwilling to do so.

The style to adopt here is known as 'participating'. At this level relationship behaviour is high and task behaviour is low. This means you share ideas and facilitate the decision making of the team. You're involved in plenty of two-way communication to get people to start taking more responsibility for the task.

R4 – This indicates high follower readiness. It means the team is both able and willing or able and confident. In both cases the team is capable and committed to the task.

This style is known as 'delegating'. You provide little direction and only a low level of support. The team is ready to take on most of the responsibility themselves, while you provide encouragement and support only when requested.

This is shown in Figure 2.2.

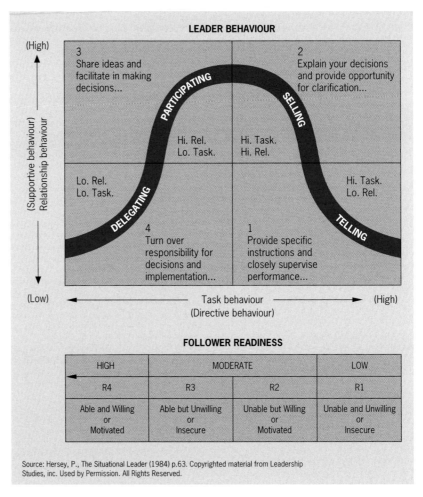

LEADER BEHAVIOUR

Source: Hersey, P., The Situational Leader (1984) p.63. Copyrighted material from Leadership Studies, inc. Used by Permission. All Rights Reserved.

Figure 2.2 *Situational leadership*   Source: *Hersey* (1984)

Situational leadership – the issues

The success or otherwise of applying situational leadership depends on your ability to be flexible in your leadership style. If you're not, you might only be effective in certain situations. Using situational leadership successfully also depends on the ability of your team to move from one situation to another. For example, they may become stuck in a particular way of doing things and fail to mature. Situational leadership also seems to assume that all team members move together as a team. What happens if the team is apparently ready to move on, apart from one or two individuals? This is not made clear.

You will also have to consider whether all four styles of leadership are available to you. For example, if you are working at quite a low level you may not be in a position to use a telling style of management. You may have to rely on gentle persuasion instead. On the other hand, if you're working in an organisational culture that emphasises the importance of management decision making and directing others, you may find it difficult to adopt a delegating style.

The idea that the situation plays an important part in leadership style provides a dynamic and flexible view of leadership rather than a static one, which suits the modern approach to management and corporate culture.

Source: *Hannagan* (1998)

The model has, however, come in for some criticism.

Counter argument

Criticisms of situational leadership

It is inconsistent in the way it connects concern for the task/relationship with ability/willingness. The development level continuum lacks continuity since it requires willingness to appear, disappear and reappear as the development level increases. Finally, it runs counter to conformity in that it does not start with a style of high risk and high relationship for a group, which is simultaneously unable and unwilling.

Source: *Nicholls quoted by Mullins* (1996)

Supportive argument

In support of situational leadership

Some people have difficulty understanding the development of followers from R1, R2 and R3. How can one go from being insecure to confident and then become insecure again? The important thing to remember is that at the lower level of readiness, the leader is providing the direction – the what, where, when and how. Therefore the decisions are leader-directed. At the highest level of readiness, followers become responsible for tasks direction, and the decisions are follower-directed. This transition from leader-directed to follower-directed may result in apprehension or insecurity. As followers move from low levels of readiness to higher levels, the combinations of task and relationship behaviour appropriate to the situation begin to change.

Source: *Hersey quoted by Mullins* (1996)

Activity 6
Situational leadership in action

Objective

This activity will help you to apply situational leadership in work scenarios.

Task

Use the situational leadership model to help you decide which of the styles would be the most appropriate to use in each of these four situations. Give a reason for your answer in each case.

1   You manage a team in a call centre. Your team takes calls from small shopkeepers enquiring about the new product lines that you sell. Its role is to keep customers updated on new lines and to take orders. News has filtered through to you that they are failing to do this.

How would you tackle this?

2   You have assigned the induction of a new starter to a member of your team who has the knowledge, skills and enthusiasm to carry out the role properly. You have to spend time with the experienced team member to establish the outcomes you expect and the timescales required.

What style might you adopt?

3   A machinery breakdown means that one area of your production is halted. The implication is that schedules are delayed, and this has a knock-on effect in terms of delivery of orders. You also suspect that the problem arose through carelessness or misuse, rather than poor maintenance.

What would you do?

4 As a development exercise, you have asked two members of your team to produce a report for your senior manager. They have a week to produce the report, plus a PowerPoint presentation. On the second day you check how it's going and find no progress has been made.

What style would you use?

Now identify four work situations of your own where you might use each of the styles of situational leadership.

Feedback

See how far your ideas for each of the four scenarios agrees with these suggestions.

1 This could be a situation for either telling or, more likely, selling. They will certainly need direction in the task. You will also need to find out whether it is unwillingness or lack of ability to do what they should before you decide which style to adopt.

2 This is a case for delegating, as the team member is both able and confident enough to carry out the induction role.

3 The machine breakdown is definitely a case for telling. There has to be a heavy emphasis on task because of the knock-on effects. To put it bluntly, the mistake should never have happened in the first place.

4 The style you will adopt with the team members is likely to be participating. However, if it goes on for much longer, you'll have to sell, perhaps even tell. They should be able to carry out the task – the key question for you is: how willing are they?

You may want to discuss your ideas for applying situational leadership in your work with your manager or a trusted colleague.

Action-centred leadership

Action-centred leadership is based on the idea that there are three areas of need within a team. These are task, individual and team maintenance needs. It is at the crossover points that your role as the leader becomes important in balancing the needs of all three. Action-centred leadership is the work of John Adair (1997).

Three areas of need

Adair symbolises the three areas of need as overlapping circles, as shown in Figure 2.3.

Figure 2.3 *Action-centred leadership*   Source: *Adair* (1997)

According to Adair's theory, the best leaders meet the needs of all three areas adequately. This means balancing task, team maintenance and individual needs effectively.

♦ Task needs are simply those activities at work that have to be completed in order to achieve the desired outcome

♦ Team maintenance needs are the things that have to be done to promote harmony and good relations within the team – for the good of the team

♦ Individual needs are the things individuals need to help them to achieve as individuals, for example praise, status or development.

These needs change according to the situation. In one situation, you may have to give more attention to the needs of the team than to the needs of the task or individuals, whereas in another you may have to place more emphasis on the needs of the task. For example, in the early stages of building a team you may need to focus heavily on the task – the main purpose of the team. This will help to provide a good foundation for the team and individuals working to achieve the task.

The key is that as the manager, you have to keep the needs of the task, the team and the individual at the forefront of your mind.

What is required of the manager to carry out this balancing act is shown in Table 2.1.

Task functions	Team functions	Individual
Achieving the objectives of the work group	Maintaining morale and building team spirit	Meeting the needs of the individual members of the group
Defining group tasks	The cohesiveness of the group as a working unit	Attending to personal problems
Planning the work		Giving praise and status
Allocation of resources	Setting standards and maintaining discipline	Reconciling conflicts between group needs and the needs of the individual
Organisation of duties and responsibilities	Systems of communication within the group	Training the individual
Controlling quality and checking performance	Training the group	
Reviewing progress	Appropriateness of sub-leaders	

Table 2.1 *The manager's role*   Source: *Mullins* (1996)

The three-circle approach used by Adair serves to illustrate the close relationship between leadership and management. Building the team and satisfying individual needs would include leadership. Achieving the common task clearly involves the process of management.

Source: *Mullins* (1996)

How can this help me?

If you are relatively new to management, this is a useful model to follow. It gives some structure to your work and stops you from trying to do it all. Adair points out that if you can learn the functions of leadership associated with task, team and individual, it is your entrance door to effective leadership. Practice, experience and reflection will help you carry out these functions with skill. In other words, functions are associated with doing and they have an underlying skill set that can be learned. This then becomes your toolbox of leadership skills.

The functions he lists are given below, with examples of the skills that can be learned. What is interesting is that while these functions would all seem to lie in the task circle of Adair's model, they are all fundamental to keeping the needs of the three circles in balance. In other words, the skills you learn can be used in any circumstances.

Defining the task means deciding what it is that has to be achieved that gives the team a sense of direction.

This can help you to learn how to:

◆ set clear objectives

◆ question why, not just what

◆ relate your team's tasks to the wider aims of the organisation

◆ think in abstract (strategic) terms, not just in concrete (operational) terms.

Planning is about putting in place actions to take you from where you are now to where you want to be, that is, achieving your objectives.

The skills involved might be:

◆ asking questions about how, when and who

◆ sharing information

◆ sharing decision making

◆ being adaptable when plans must change.

Briefing means communicating objectives and plans to the team.

This will help you to:

- give effective presentations
- brief others
- listen actively
- explain things in different ways.

Controlling means making sure the team is on course to achieve the objectives.

The skills you will learn include:

- monitoring performance
- using resources effectively
- dealing with problems
- using creativity.

Evaluating is about checking that the work achieves the objective that is agreed, that is, measuring progress against your success criteria.

This will help you to:

- appraise performance
- give feedback
- deal with under-performance in a constructive way
- provide recognition for a job well done.

Motivating others to maintain high levels of performance throughout.

You can learn to:

- find out about individual needs
- reward people appropriately
- build team morale through a variety of strategies
- build team cohesion.

Organising is to do with structuring and restructuring as required.

So, for example, you can learn how to:

- work within organisational systems
- build and maintain the team as an effective unit
- delegate work to others
- manage your time.

Providing an example means setting a good example for your team.

The skills you can learn are:

◆ self-discipline and self-management

◆ learning from others

◆ empowering others

◆ 'do as I do' rather than 'do as I say'.

The danger of not learning the lessons of leadership

Mr Big never feels comfortable unless in total control. Mr Big likes to know everything that is going on, while, by contrast, others around Mr Big are left in the dark and spend part of their time guessing. Mr Big shows equal interest in the strategic side of the business and the operational side. Nothing is allowed to escape his gaze. As a result Mr Big is overworked. The fact that Mr Big is a workaholic and often arrives at the office before anyone else would appear to be an adaptation to the intensities of the workload. But the harder Mr Big works, the greater the workload becomes. That is because Mr Big generates much work for his staff. The outcomes of his briefings and instructions then need to be supervised, for Mr Big refuses to believe that others can be left on their own and are bright enough to make the right decisions.

Source: *Belbin* (1996)

Activity 7
Action-centred leadership and you

Objective

This activity will help you to analyse how well you fulfil the role of the action-centred leader by meeting the needs of the task, the team and the individual.

Task

The following checklist covers the three areas of action-centred leadership. Tick the boxes where you can answer 'yes' to each question. Put a cross in the boxes where you have to answer 'no' to a question, and bear in mind that some questions are in two parts.

It would also be helpful to get the opinions of some of your team.

Achieving the task		Yes	No
Purpose	Am I clear what my task is?	☐	☐
Responsibilities	Am I clear what my responsibilities are?	☐	☐
Objectives	Have I agreed objectives with my superior?	☐	☐
Working conditions	Are these right for the group?	☐	☐
Resources	Is there adequate authority, money and materials?	☐	☐
Targets	Does each member have clearly defined and agreed targets?	☐	☐
Authority	Is the line of authority clear?	☐	☐
Training	Are there any gaps in specialist skills or in the abilities of individuals in the group which are required for the task?	☐	☐
Priorities	Have I planned the time effectively?	☐	☐
Progress	Do I make regular checks and evaluate progress?	☐	☐
Supervision	In case of my absence, is it clear who covers for me?	☐	☐
Example	Do I set standards by my behaviour?	☐	☐

Building and maintaining the team		Yes	No
Objectives	Does the team clearly understand and accept them?	☐	☐
Standards	Do they know what standards of performance are expected?	☐	☐
Safety standards	Do they know the consequences of infringement?	☐	☐
Size of team	Is the size correct?	☐	☐
Team members	Are the right people working together?	☐	☐
Team spirit	Do I look for opportunities for building the concept of teamwork into jobs?	☐	☐
Discipline	Are the rules seen to be reasonable?	☐	☐
	Am I fair and impartial in enforcing them?	☐	☐
Grievances	Are grievances dealt with promptly? Do I take action on matters likely to disrupt the group?	☐	☐
Consultation	Is this genuine?	☐	☐
	Do I encourage and welcome ideas and suggestions?	☐	☐
Briefing	Is this regular?	☐	☐
	Does it cover current plans, progress and future developments?	☐	☐
Represent	Am I prepared to represent and champion the feelings of the group when required?	☐	☐
Support	Do I visit people at their work when the team is apart?	☐	☐
	Do I then represent, to the individual, the concept of the whole team in my manner and encouragement?	☐	☐

Developing the individual		Yes	No
Targets	Have they been agreed and quantified?	☐	☐
Induction	Does the individual really know the other team members and the organisation?	☐	☐
Achievement	Does the individual know how their work contributes to the overall result?	☐	☐
Responsibilities	Is there a clear job description?	☐	☐
	Can I delegate more to the individual?	☐	☐
Authority	Does the individual have sufficient authority to achieve their task?	☐	☐
Training	Has adequate provision been made for training and retraining team members?	☐	☐

47

Developing the individual (continued)		Yes	No
Recognition	Do I emphasise people's success?	☐	☐
	In failure, is criticism constructive?	☐	☐
Growth	Does the individual see a chance of development?	☐	☐
	Is there a career path?	☐	☐
Performance	Is this regularly reviewed?	☐	☐
Reward	Are work, capacity (ability) and pay in balance?	☐	☐
The task	Is the individual right for the job?	☐	☐
	Do they have the necessary resources?	☐	☐
The person	Do I know this person well?	☐	☐
	What makes the individual different from others?	☐	☐
Time/attention	Do I spend enough time with individuals — listening, developing and counselling?	☐	☐
Grievances	Are these dealt with promptly?	☐	☐
Security	Does the individual know about pensions, redundancy and so on?	☐	☐
Appraisal	Is the overall performance of each individual regularly reviewed in face-to-face discussions?	☐	☐

Source: *Adair* (1997)

Feedback

That is a lengthy list and you probably couldn't tick every question. It is also a diverse set of questions. Some are quite straightforward to answer, such as: 'Have targets been agreed and quantified?' Others are far more complex and may take a good deal of research before you can come up with a realistic answer. For example: 'Are work, capacity (ability) and pay in balance?'

To be an action-centred leader, what you're aiming for is a dynamic balance between the task, the team and the individual. You need to give the required amount of attention in the appropriate area, depending on the situation that you are dealing with at any particular time. This is because the three areas overlap. For example, by focusing on the task at hand you can help the team to develop and help satisfy the needs of the individuals within it. On the other hand, if the team is not well maintained, this can have a harmful effect on how well the task is completed, it can damage the team and also reduce the satisfaction of the individual team members.

To make improvements in your own performance as a leader, you need to be able to attend to all three areas of need – task, team and individual. Look back at your responses to the activity and identify the area where you have placed most crosses. What action can you take to develop in this area? You may find it helpful to consult with your manager or colleagues, and then draw up an action plan to develop your skills.

◆ Recap

Determine why leadership is a requirement of modern management

◆ Leaders are typically portrayed as inspiring visionaries who are able to influence the behaviour of others, whereas managers are seen as planners, organisers and controllers. The key distinguishing feature is orientation to change.

◆ In practice the roles overlap and to be effective in today's turbulent working environment, a manager needs to develop leadership qualities.

Review contemporary developments in the field of leadership

◆ Leadership thinking has developed over the years from the trait approach, which proposes that leaders are born, through the behavioural approaches, which set out leadership qualities that can be learnt, to the contingency theorist's idea of flexible and situational leadership.

◆ Another important trend is transformational leadership which recognises the importance of leaders who are charismatic, visionary and able to win the hearts and minds of people.

Understand why effective leaders adapt their style to fit the situational context

◆ Situational leadership suggests that the manager should use telling, selling, participating and delegating styles depending on the nature of the task and the readiness of the employee.

◆ At lower levels of employee readiness, decisions are leader-led, providing support and direction, whereas at higher levels, decisions become more follower directed, promoting greater commitment and increased job satisfaction.

Explore the three areas of need within a team

◆ In his theory of action-centred leadership, Adair (1997) highlights three areas of need within a team: the needs of the task, the need to build the team and the need to satisfy individuals.

◆ Managers must meet the needs of all three areas and recognise that the balance of need will change according to the situation.

►► **More @**

Adair, J. (1987) *Effective Teambuilding: How to Make a Winning Team*, **Pan**
Explore Adair's model of action-centred leadership.

Hersey, P. (1992) *The Situational Leader,* **Pfeiffer and Co**
This book explains the Situational Leadership® Model through a realistic conversation between two managers. See also the **Centre for Leadership Studies** website, www.situational.com.

Van Maurik, J. (2004) *Writers on Leadership,* **Penguin Business**
This text synthesises the wealth of literature on leadership and provides a clear and concise overview of the major trends which have emerged over the past 100 years.

Bennis, W. (1998) *On Becoming a Leader,* **Arrow Business Books**
Based on interview with leaders, this is an account of how people become leaders, how they lead and how organisations encourage or stifle potential leaders.

Goleman, D., Boyatzis, R. and McKee, A. (2002) *The New Leaders: Transforming the Art of Leadership into the Science of Results,* **Little Brown**
From the originator of emotional intelligence, this book proposes that the new leader excels in the art of relationship – expertise which the changing business climate renders indispensable.

3 Leadership in practice

Attitudes to work and employment have changed in recent years and employees now expect more participation in management decisions and opportunities for self-development. This trend has implications for the approach of the leader and for the skills that they need.

Ethics is another social factor that is having an impact. Living socially responsible values with its people and in its marketplace and environment is now seen as vitally important for organisations that wish to enhance and protect their corporate reputation.

This theme explores critical leadership skills and values. You will:

◆ **Explore the skills required to win people's support for your leadership**

◆ **Consider why social responsibility and ethical leadership are issues of growing importance.**

The changing profile of leadership

As a manager, you need to work more closely with your team than ever before. You need to gain their commitment and manage through influence (sell) rather than through authority (tell). It requires strong communication and people skills so that, as a team, you are working towards a common outcome. This moves you away from the old management style of directing people in exactly what to do and how to do it. The result is your responsibility; the method of achieving it lies with the team.

But why is this so? Why the change of emphasis?

In an environment of change it is impossible for you to direct the work of each team member. In this climate it is better to aid team members to deal with day-to-day situations, rather than dictating to them. With changing team structures, you probably have little choice apart from influencing their general approach. The growth in cross-functional, virtual and a range of other types of team makes direct control impossible. These teams can be made up of people from a range of disciplines. You cannot hope to be an expert in all fields, so you cannot tell people how to do everything.

The need for improved customer service continues apace – whether these customers are external or internal. It is difficult for your team to respond to their changing needs if they must wait for you to tell them how to act. It is far better to let them act in the way they see best. So again, your role becomes one of influence. Not only does this mean the customer is likely to receive a better standard of service, it can also mean improved job satisfaction. Giving control to team members can make work more challenging and satisfying.

So what does a manager need in order to put this sell rather than tell approach into practice? We will consider this now.

A focus on people skills

There is a growing trend towards the development of management/leadership competencies. This is useful because competence is a way of describing management across a variety of functions. This approach acknowledges that your role, by its very nature, can change rapidly.

Table 3.1 is a result of research among managers in the private and public sectors in the UK. It highlights which competencies the managers themselves would rate most highly.

Competency	Percentage regarding this as important
Teamworking	70
People management	69
Communication	69
Leadership	59
Problem solving	59
Planning and organising	59
Interpersonal skills	56
Motivating others	54
Decision making	51
Commercial awareness	34
Project working	24

Table 3.1 *Competency ratings by managers*

Source: *The Industrial Society* (1996)

It is an interesting list. This is because while it includes some functional competencies such as project work and commercial awareness, these are rated as far less important than people skills, such as teamwork and communication.

Here is another list, where the focus on people skills is just as strong and there is also an emphasis on managing oneself:

1 Listens carefully to others.

2 Gives people responsibility for tasks and projects.

3 Challenges the rules and conventions of the organisation.

4 Has a clear vision for the team.

5 Has a clear perception of own strengths and weaknesses.

6 Encourages ideas from the team.

7 Demonstrates trust to others.

8 Anticipates and adapts to changing conditions.

9 Communicates the vision and ideas clearly to others.

10 Spends time keeping up-to-date and developing new skills.

11 Motivates and encourages others.

12 Provides training to enable people to work effectively.

13 Helps others to manage change.

14 Demonstrates a high level of commitment to own work.

15 Manages time well.

16 Develops a good communication network throughout the organisation.

17 Provides support for people when needed.

18 Manages stress well.

19 Focuses on achieving results.

20 Has a positive attitude towards self.

Source: *Jones et al.* (1996)

The list of competencies is potentially endless. However, they are a useful way of looking at the requirements of leadership, because they can combine activities, skills and behaviours in a way which otherwise may be difficult.

There is another competency that may be important for those in a leadership role and that is emotional intelligence. This is the way both you and the people on your team understand, manage and control your emotions. If you understand that a person's ability to handle their emotions is an important factor in how they perform at work, and handle aspects of their work involving things like stress, you are in a better position to manage them.

Emotional intelligence is an increasingly important feature for leaders today as so much of their work is based on activities that actually appeal to people's emotions. It is to do with empathising with people, rather than seeing things from one point of view. It is to do with helping people to get along well with one another at work, and it is to do with being able to persuade and influence others.

Using influence and persuasion

As you have seen, influence and persuasion are key components of the 'sell' rather than 'tell' approach. They are also very important to leaders who may lack the authority or status of an important job title – if you have the ability to influence, you don't always need the power. Influence and persuasion can be useful when you are:

♦ trying to get a team member to take a particular course of action

♦ obtaining more resources for your team

♦ getting a team member to see your point of view or change their own views

♦ requiring team members to work more effectively together

♦ needing someone on the team to take more ownership of a situation

♦ asking someone to work harder to get a piece of work completed.

The stages in influencing others:

♦ Decide what you want to achieve – what is your objective?

♦ Decide what tactic you are going to use – this may differ depending on whether you're dealing with a group or an individual

♦ Think about what objections may arise – and come up with tactics to overcome these objections

♦ Work out a fall-back position – the least you will accept

♦ Build empathy with the other person – see things from their point of view

♦ State your case clearly and confidently – giving reasons why

♦ Stay positive – you're more likely to trigger a positive response

♦ Listen and give credit for any relevant suggestions

♦ Incorporate good ideas into your final plan

♦ Evaluate how it went and learn from your mistakes.

Of course there may not always be time to use influencing or persuading skills. There may be cases when it's just not appropriate, such as a major customer complaint when a member of the team was clearly in the wrong. However, using these skills is the best way to build commitment in the long term – by persuading people to see the logic in your case. If the other parties feel involved and have the chance to think things through, they are more likely to be won over in the end and for the long term.

Activity 8
Leadership attributes

Objective

Use this activity to consider a model for leadership and its related leadership competencies.

Task

Read the following article about leadership at Xerox.

Under the leadership of Fournier, who became chief executive in 1989, [the company] developed the Xerox management model (see below), to focus efforts on winning the European Quality Award. This also proved helpful during the re-engineering phase [i.e. during a period of massive change] by giving the customer business units a common purpose.

Used in conjunction with the Xerox management model are two checklists of the skills and behaviours that the company aims to develop and encourage. These comprise 23 leadership attributes, which others might refer to as competencies, and nine cultural dimensions, against which all senior managers are assessed each year (see below).

Each of the '23+9' as they are usually referred to, is divided into a number of criteria. For example, on the leadership attribute referring to 'cross-functional teamwork', managers are judged according to whether they:

♦ understand the roles and responsibilities of functions and divisions, and how they can work across boundaries

♦ maintain close relationships across organisational boundaries to achieve policy deployment/business results

♦ recognise diverse stakeholder needs and gain support for shared goals

♦ negotiate and implement work processes across the boundaries.

In the same way, the cultural dimension for 'open and honest communication' requires managers to be assessed on whether they:

♦ are sensitive to the concerns and feelings of others

♦ do not treat disagreement as disloyalty

♦ foster feedback, dialogue and information sharing

♦ encourage openness through personal behaviour

♦ confront conflict openly.

Of course, not all the 23+9 are equally important to all managers. Jobs at different levels and in different specialisms will prioritise different bundles of leadership attributes. But the framework provides a clear picture of the ideal, rounded Xerox manager, and all employees are asked each year to assess their managers against it as part of a 360-degree appraisal process. The framework is then used to focus individuals' development plans and the company's succession plan.

Source: *MacLachlan* (1998)

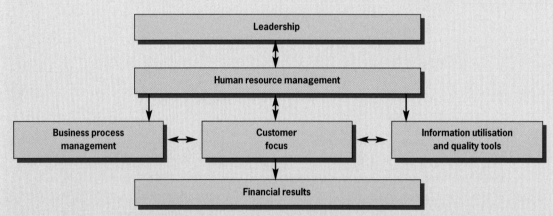

Figure 3.1 *The Xerox management model*

The 23 leadership attributes	*The 9 cultural dimensions*
1 Strategic thinking	1 Market connected
2 Strategic implementation	2 Absolute results orientated
3 Customer-driven approach	3 Action orientated
4 Inspiring a shared vision	4 Line driven
5 Decision-making	5 Team orientated
6 Quick study	6 Empowered people
7 Managing operational performance	7 Open and honest communication
8 Staffing for high performance	8 Organisation reflection and learning
9 Developing organisational talent	9 Process re-engineering and simplification
10 Delegation and empowerment	
11 Managing teamwork	
12 Cross functional teamwork	
13 Leading innovation	
14 Drives for business results	
15 Use of 'leadership through quality'	
16 Openness to change	
17 Interpersonal empathy and understanding	
18 Personal drive	
19 Personal strength and maturity	
20 Personal consistency	
21 Environment and industry perspective	
22 Business and financial perspective	
23 Overall technical knowledge	

Table 3.2 *23+9*   Source: *MacLachlan* (1998)

1 How does the Xerox management model empower its people to focus on the needs of its customers?

List your answers here:

2 How is this emphasis on people management reflected in the 23+9 formula?

List your answers here:

Feedback

1 The model concentrates on leadership in relation to human resource (HR) management. If the management of HR is effective, people are then able to manage business processes, and information and quality tools in order to meet the needs of the customers directly. This then results in the desired financial results.

2 Many of the attributes are to do with the people skills of management, rather than those that are operationally driven. Clearly attributes such as 'overall technical knowledge' (23) and 'strategic implementation' (2) are important, but many of the other attributes relate to managing people, such as 'developing organisational talent' (9), 'delegation and empowerment' (10), interpersonal empathy and understanding' (17).

Activity 9
Looking at your leadership skills

Objective

This activity will help you to review your leadership skills and consider ways of making improvements.

Task

The following list contains the key skills and qualities of an effective leader, some of which you may recognise from other activities you have completed on team leadership. Use the list to analyse your own skill level by giving yourself a rating for each skill/quality.

Next to each statement the ratings are marked one to four. These signify a sliding scale.

1 = totally underdeveloped

2 = significantly underdeveloped

3 = satisfactory

4 = fully developed

If you have no experience at all in any particular area, then leave the column blank. However, if you don't use these skills in your present job, it doesn't matter. Draw on your experiences in other jobs and the activities you undertake outside work.

Once complete, ask your manager, or a colleague who knows you well, to assess your skills by completing the chart with a pen in a different colour. (Or you could photocopy the chart so you each complete a blank one.) Then come together to assess the results and reach a consensus score of 1, 2, 3 or 4. Write this in your 'overall score'.

	Rating	Overall score
Understanding how the team's role fits in with the organisation's objectives	1 2 3 4	
Sharing the organisation/team vision with others	1 2 3 4	
Setting own goals and objectives	1 2 3 4	
Working with team members to set their goals and objectives	1 2 3 4	
Following relevant organisational systems and procedures	1 2 3 4	
Knowing what motivates different members of the team	1 2 3 4	
Being flexible in dealing with different people	1 2 3 4	
Making and using contacts in different areas of the business	1 2 3 4	
Managing time to set priorities and get tasks done	1 2 3 4	
Being seen as approachable by own and other departments	1 2 3 4	

	Rating	Overall score
Delegating tasks to others	1 2 3 4	
Empowering others	1 2 3 4	
Trusting others to complete a job properly	1 2 3 4	
Expressing praise and giving constructive criticism	1 2 3 4	
Sharing credit with the team when things go well	1 2 3 4	
Stimulating enthusiasm in colleagues and team members	1 2 3 4	
Developing own skills and knowledge	1 2 3 4	
Communicating clearly with people at different levels within the organisation	1 2 3 4	
Adapting to change when the business requires it	1 2 3 4	
Explaining difficult ideas to others	1 2 3 4	
Keeping your line manager informed on a regular basis	1 2 3 4	
Putting own ideas forward assertively	1 2 3 4	
Changing your mind in the light of new or better information	1 2 3 4	
Using and interpreting body language effectively	1 2 3 4	
Influencing the ideas and opinions of others	1 2 3 4	
Recommending improvements to work systems and operations	1 2 3 4	
Managing meetings well	1 2 3 4	
Giving people the opportunity to discuss problems that may/may not be work based	1 2 3 4	
Providing the resources people need to do their jobs well	1 2 3 4	
Appraising the performance of individuals on the team regularly	1 2 3 4	
Helping individuals to plan their own development	1 2 3 4	
Linking training and development to the needs of the business	1 2 3 4	
Handling information in confidence and with tact	1 2 3 4	
Asking open questions to obtain all the information required	1 2 3 4	
Summarising and reflecting the details of a discussion	1 2 3 4	
Listening actively to what others say	1 2 3 4	
Building rapport with individuals	1 2 3 4	
Planning and organising an event or activity	1 2 3 4	
Solving arguments and disputes within the team	1 2 3 4	
Sizing up a situation quickly to identify the source of a problem	1 2 3 4	
Persuading others to see my point of view	1 2 3 4	
Involving others in decision making	1 2 3 4	
Negotiating with others to find the best way forward	1 2 3 4	
Taking difficult decisions when consensus cannot be reached	1 2 3 4	
Remaining calm and in control during a crisis	1 2 3 4	
Dealing with the negative reactions of others	1 2 3 4	

	Rating	Overall score
Thinking on my feet to solve a particular difficulty	1 2 3 4	
Communicating clearly to a group of people	1 2 3 4	
Backing up ideas with supporting facts and evidence	1 2 3 4	
Engendering enthusiasm and commitment in other people	1 2 3 4	

Feedback

When you have agreed an overall score for each item with your manager, have a look at those items where you have scored 1 or 2.

See if any pattern emerges, for example, are your low scores to do with communication, using systems and procedures or dealing with difficult situations?

Talk to your manager and agree what actions you can take to help improve the areas that are currently underdeveloped.

Ethical leadership – a new way forward

Being socially responsible is an important issue for many organisations today. This means some businesses are looking beyond the needs of their shareholders and looking at the people and the environment that they affect.

What do we mean by ethical leadership?

Social responsibility is good for business. A survey carried out with 100 managers and directors points to this fact (see Table 3.3). It seems there needs to be a balancing act between producing returns for shareholders and being responsible towards employees, the environment, the community and society at large. They are all stakeholders in the organisation – people and external bodies that have an interest in how the organisation performs and the way it conducts its business.

	Strongly agree	Agree	Neutral	Disagree	Strongly disagree
The primary goal of any business should be to remain profitable over the long term in order to produce returns for shareholders	25	53	10	11	2
The only social responsibility of business is wealth creation	1	12	14	55	19
Part of doing good business is taking responsibility for the impact of your activities on the natural environment.	32	60	7	1	0
Business decision makers have a responsibility to take into account the impact of decisions on the communities in which they operate	28	59	7	4	1
Organisations can differentiate themselves in the market place by demonstrating social responsibility in the way they do business	37	50	11	2	1
Business should seek to act in the best interests of the wider society	9	65	19	6	0

Table 3.3 *Social responsibility survey highlights (showing %)*

Source: *Butcher and Harvey* (1999)

Are both things possible – social responsibility and profit? It would seem the answer is yes, so far as the current success of so-called ethical funds and businesses is concerned. It seems that they, above all others, can ride the ups and downs of the stock market. This situation makes them attractive to potential shareholders.

Therefore, with the possibility for higher future investment, such companies look set to flourish, and others will join this trend as the potential for increased profit improves.

So how does this affect you as a manager?

It probably means a requirement to adopt the practices of ethical management – if you don't already do so. It may be that you as an individual can do little to influence the strategic position of the company. For example, where and how it obtains its raw materials, what production methods are used or to what markets to sell its goods.

Where you can have an effect is most certainly the way you manage your people and the personal example you set. Ethical leadership is about fair, just and equitable treatment for all staff. This helps build a relationship of trust, which may well have been damaged over recent years with redundancy and loss of job security. It helps build commitment to you personally and to the organisation.

Building a partnership with employees means treating them fairly in terms of the opportunities they have for development, promoting an atmosphere of openness and listening to their ideas and opinions. It also means that you ensure company policies and procedures are applied fairly. This in turn has a positive effect on customer loyalty as customers receive better service from people who themselves are treated well.

On the wider front, when there is little to choose between the products and services of different businesses, customers will look at other factors before making a choice. One of those factors is the culture and values of the organisation. These are often reflected, very publicly, in how an organisation does business. For example, a company using child labour, using animals in experiments or causing an environmental disaster will lose more customers than it gains. Such events are guaranteed to reach the public eye and result in a loss of reputation that can last for years.

Redefining business, refocusing management

Firms such as BP, BT and Shell are producing reports that emphasise their contribution to society. Accountants are working on a social and ethical accounting model, amid talk of moving towards a 'triple bottom line'. Ethical investment funds have been growing throughout the 1990s, and the new Pensions Act will require pension trustees to state their ethical stance.

These activities recognise the growing interdependence of business and society, and the potential convergence of interests in the long term. It implies a redefinition of the managerial role to that of a custodian of resources for the public good. It would, in many cases, mean an important shift in personal orientation. Managers might then see themselves less as a powerful, well-rewarded elite and more as 'leader-servants' to others.

Source: *Butcher and Harvey* (1999)

The ethical manager in action

...the emphasis is as much on who you are as what you do. It's what Stephen Covey, in his enormously successful and influential book *The Seven Habits of Highly Successful People* calls the character ethics. Leadership isn't just about a set of behaviours; it's about the kind of person you are inside. Leadership is about personal integrity, trust and credibility...this change reflects the business environment.

Source: *Reynolds* (2000)

The basic principles of ethical leadership involve being open and honest in your dealings with your staff and displaying appropriate behaviours. As Stephen Covey says: *'You can't talk your way out of something you behaved your way into.'*

It involves being consistent in the way that you treat them. This is not the same as treating everyone the same. In fact, it may mean the opposite as you are dealing with individuals who have different needs and different characteristics.

Ethical management also means using your power for the good of the team – rather than as a means of control or for personal gain. Your use of power needs to be controlled, disciplined and focused – towards achieving targets, building the team and empowering individuals. In other words, your power is used in the three main areas of task, team and individual of John Adair's action-centred leadership.

Using power in an ethical way

If your power as a leader is being used properly you should be:

- building bridges across the organisation – up, down and sideways
- demonstrating support for others
- acting as an ambassador – standing up for your team and their needs
- making sure everyone has a common commitment to a clear goal
- ensuring everyone is treated in a fair and equitable way – from the strongest to the weakest.

You may face problems if two sets of opposing forces work on each other. On the one hand, you believe in ethical leadership, while on the other you're being driven to meet ever-higher targets and more challenging objectives. If this is a dilemma for you, the crux of the issue lies around how you use your power.

You can use it to coerce others into action, but this will bring only short-term gains. People will do what they are told – but only once. Next time you'll have to push that bit harder to get them to perform. On the other hand, if you use power properly, in an ethical way, it may seem harder at the beginning, but is almost guaranteed to bring better long-term results. In fact, this is at the heart of the socially responsible organisation – sacrificing short-term gain for long-term business performance and reputation.

Activity 10
Ethical leadership

Objective

This activity will help you to consider how an ethical approach to working can be good for business.

As more and more businesses talk in terms of ethical policies and practices, it is important to understand what might be considered ethical and what might not.

Case study

Read the following article from *The Sunday Times* in 2001.

Mr Sam: the folksy tycoon with a killer instinct

By the time of his death in 1992, Sam Walton had amassed one of the greatest fortunes in American history and today his family is the richest in the world, with a fortune of $45 billion.

Walton opened his first shop in 1945 with the aid of a $25,000 loan from his father-in-law, going it alone to open his first Wal-Mart store in 1962.

Walton's philosophy – the one Wal-Mart lives by today – was to buy cheap and sell cheap, letting sales rather than profit margins drive the firm. His relentless cost-cutting started at home with his car and spread to the business, with his insistence that, for example, all staff fly economy class. It has gone on to have profound effects across the world.

Wal-Mart's drive for ever cheaper products has led to huge swathes of manufacturing moving overseas. The company has been accused of using suppliers that employ children and inflict inhumane conditions on their workers.

At the same time Wal-Mart's huge stores and rock bottom prices have forced smaller competitors out of business. There is little in the way of local shops in Bentonville, where Wal-Mart has its headquarters, and that has set a pattern across the United States.

The antithesis of the archetypical remote tycoon, Walton kept his telephone number listed in the local directory and would often drop into stores or depots to chat with staff. In 1984, after Wal-Mart's profits exceeded expectation, he did a Hawaiian hula dance in the middle of Wall Street to celebrate.

But behind the folksy image lay a cut-throat businessman. Unions that tried to organise Wal-Mart's staff were crushed and manufacturers that could not cut their costs were ditched. At the

same time that Wal-Mart was running a 'Buy America'
campaign, it had become the country's largest importer of goods
from China.

Source: *Rushe* (2001)

Task

Now answer the following questions.

1 What evidence is provided in the case study that Wal-Mart has
taken a far from ethical approach in some of its business dealings?

Evidence of unethical business dealings:

2 Clearly the consumer is benefiting from low prices in Wal-Mart
stores. Do you believe the consumer will be the winner in the long
run? Give reasons for your answer.

Reasons why I believe the consumer will/will not be the winner:

3 Are there signs within society that ethics is becoming a concern for
consumers, which could cause a backlash against organisations of
this kind?

Signs within society of a backlash against organisations of this kind:

4 Think of examples of organisations that you consider have combined an ethical approach to leadership with profitability. This may include your own organisation.

What factors indicate to you that they are an ethical organisation?

Feedback

Your ideas may include the following:

1 According to *The Sunday Times* article, the company has acted locally and globally in a number of ways that can be seen as unethical. For example:

   ◆ not allowing staff access to trade union membership

   ◆ ditching manufacturers which could not cut costs

   ◆ moving manufacturing abroad

   ◆ possibly using manufacturers that employ child labour and those that impose inhumane working conditions

   ◆ importing goods from China during a 'Buy America' campaign

   ◆ putting out of business small, local stores which could not compete on price.

2 Only time will tell whether the consumer will be the winner in the long run. There is clearly a danger that if an organisation the size of Wal-Mart does succeed in its plans to dominate world retailing of this kind, it will have a monopoly as other retailers are put out of business. The danger with this from the consumer's point of view is that once competition is eliminated, Wal-Mart can increase prices without fear of being undercut.

3 There are signs that people are becoming concerned about ethics. Bad publicity, especially in the US, about the use of child labour and poor working conditions by Gap and Nike in the late 1990s are indicators of this. Whether this will affect Wal-Mart is yet to be seen. Another article about Wal-Mart in the same newspaper does say that 'outside the business community Wal-Mart is in danger of becoming a public enemy, accused of sucking the life out of small communities, with its huge edge-of-town stores'. Perhaps a backlash has begun. What is interesting about ethics is that it tends to be culturally specific. Therefore, what may be acceptable in the

United States may not be the case in Europe as Wal-Mart tries to expand its business success throughout the world via the European route.

4 Common themes across ethical organisations include the following. They tend to:

- ◆ treat staff well and provide them with a safe working environment and a fair wage

- ◆ look after the environment, or at least do nothing to actively damage it

- ◆ avoid using suppliers who exploit workers or use child labour, and take social responsibility for improving the work/life conditions in those countries in which they work

- ◆ be scandal free – in terms of how their leaders behave and their attitude towards government, for example, they would never be involved in corruption

- ◆ listen to their customers' views

- ◆ balance the needs of shareholders with the way they treat staff, suppliers and customers

- ◆ expect their managers and staff to 'live and breathe' the ethical values that the organisation believes are important

- ◆ establish policies, procedures and codes of practice to reinforce their beliefs.

Activity 11
Leadership styles in difficult situations

Objective

This activity will help you to consider how working conditions affect management style.

One could argue that it is easier to be a participative and ethical leader when 'times are good'. Is it therefore likely that when conditions are difficult, the opposite is true?

Task

Read the following extracts, which highlight very different approaches to leadership in difficult times.

No more Mr Nice Guy

Towards the end of this time (Margaret Thatcher was the Prime Minister of the UK), and in the early years of the Blair government a new, more harmonious mood developed in industry. Long-term pay agreements promised job security and progressive pay rises in return for industrial peace. The power of the unions waned.

In response to this more thoughtful and progressive strain of business, leaders emerged. Captains of industry were often seen as charismatic figures. They became what Brian Baxter, senior partner at Kiddy and Partners – the business psychologists, characterises as 'all-round good guys'.

But the era of the good guy may be over. Business has never been tougher. Stock markets demand constant improvement in performance, and chief executives' heads roll with unnerving frequency. Nothing can be taken for granted.

He (Baxter) believes he has identified a new management stereotype which for convenience he has christened type A.

'Type A is a tough, driving leader. He's not really a nice sort of guy,' says Baxter. 'He's not liked or admired but he's widely respected. He knows what he's doing when things get difficult.'

Baxter continues, 'In challenging circumstances, the nurturing kind of leader, type B, is less effective. A lot of the data suggests that the A-type leader is better for business in tough times.'

Management commentators have suggested that leaders should try to combine the characteristics of type A and type B.

But Baxter, who himself was once an advocate of this, now argues that such behaviour is wrong. He says that managers who try this approach risk being accused of deviousness and often find the personal pressures insupportable. He thinks it is more effective to have a 'cleaner management model' with 'the well-balanced organisation having both types'.

Source: *Elgin* (2001)

Shackleton's lesson in leadership

After *Endurance*, Sir Edward Shackleton's Antarctic expedition ship, was crushed and sunk by the ice, he and his men were left stranded, 1,200 miles from civilisation in horrific conditions.

But, undaunted, Shackleton took his 27 men and the ship's boat, dragged them partway over the ice, camped for months and then struggled through wild seas to dismal uninhabited Elephant Island. There he left behind the main body of men, and with five companions set out on what must be the most remarkable small-boat voyage ever made: 800 miles through appalling conditions to South Georgia. Shortly afterwards he retrieved his crew.

Shackleton's skills were boundless. Painstaking attention to detail, whether in the packing of supplies on board *Endurance* or choosing the right team for each task, came naturally to him.

Unlike Robert Scott, who had the habit of blaming his crew (including Shackleton on an earlier expedition) when things went wrong, Shackleton invariably treated his men with respect and encouragement. The worst adversity left him undeterred. If his plans went wrong, he invariably had a workable plan on hand.

Source: *Elgin* (2001b)

1 Think about the descriptions of type A and type B managers in the first extract. What are the arguments for and against adopting a more authoritarian type A approach in difficult work conditions?

For type A in difficult work conditions:

Against type A in difficult work conditions:

2 Use the information in the extracts you have just read and your own knowledge on the subject to help you develop your arguments about appropriate leadership styles. Note your ideas here.

Appropriate leadership styles:

Feedback

1 Key points that you may have highlighted are as follows.

For type A in difficult work conditions:	*Against type A in difficult work conditions:*
You can get things done quickly because there is no need to involve others	People feel isolated and powerless
Crises can be handled in the way the manager sees fit	People are less likely to enter into a psychological contract with you
You can get people to do what you want as their own needs and feelings don't come into the equation	Talented people may well leave – without telling you why
You don't need to concern yourself with the ideas and opinions of the team	There is no creativity or innovation – often needed in difficult times
You give the impression of being a strong leader to the outside world, which can increase confidence in the business	Decisions are taken and problems solved on the basis of a very narrow view – the manager's
	People are confused if a type B manager reverts to type A behaviours
	People are less likely to work harder for the good of the team, as commitment is low
	Visionary and charismatic leadership will be lost

It is an interesting debate, and perhaps it is natural for managers to become more directive in difficult times. However, it seems unlikely that such a manager will have the full support and backing of the team. The manager can become isolated and while things get done more quickly, they happen in a way that stifles creativity and commitment – at the very time when these are needed most.

2 To develop your ideas you may find it helpful to discuss leadership styles with colleagues. You may also find that there is no consensus!

◆ Recap

Explore the skills required to win people's support for your leadership

◆ The skills of influencing and persuasion are core skills for leaders who can no longer rely on their position of power.

◆ Organisations commonly use competence frameworks to describe the leadership behaviours they value. Within these frameworks, people skills are consistently considered more important than process-based management skills.

Consider why social responsibility and ethical leadership are issues of growing importance

♦ There is mounting pressure on organisations to behave in a socially responsible way towards employees, the environment, the local community, customers and other stakeholders.

♦ For managers, the basic principles of ethical leadership involve being honest and open in your dealings with your team and using your power in an ethical way.

►► More @

Adair, J. (2002) *100 Greatest Ideas for Effective Leadership and Management*, **Capstone Publishing**
The book provides accessible advice from one of the world's best-known and most sought-after authorities on leadership and management – advice you can put into practice immediately.

The Management Standards Centre (MSC) – www.management-standards.org
This organisation publishes nationally agreed standards that define the level of performance expected in employment for a range of management and leadership activities.

McCann, D. (1993) *How to Influence Others at Work*, **Butterworth-Heinemann**
Develop your communication skills so that you are able to influence the outcome of conversations. See also www.tms.com.au/influencing.html

Go to the **BT Goup** website, **www.groupbt.com/society/environment/bal/ethical.htm**, for an interesting article about BT's ethics and social accountability.

Team building

It is relatively easy to establish a degree of teamwork within a group of people but infinitely harder to develop a high-performing team. Some groups seem to gel and become productive very quickly whereas others reach a plateau and for a long time hardly appear to improve at all. Some actually regress in their effectiveness.

In his book *Effective Teambuilding*, John Adair talks about the constant flux of group life:

> Not only is the group moving as a unit, but the various elements within it are constantly interacting. A change in procedure will affect the atmosphere, which will affect the participation pattern, which will affect cohesion, which will affect morale so on.

Source: *Adair* (1987)

Organisational psychologists have tried to chart the stages of group development and to discover what managers can do to move their teams quickly towards higher levels of performance. Their work is explored in this theme.

In this theme, you will:

◆ **Identify the stages of team development**

◆ **Explore strategies for developing your team towards peak performance**

◆ **Review the mix of skills and attributes required to create a fully effective team.**

Stages in team development

Teamwork is recognised as the most effective way to get things done. Teams can contribute to the organisation's success and provide support and satisfaction for the individuals within it. However, not all teams are equally capable. This is partly because of the individuals on the team and partly to do with how well developed the team is. Clearly it is critical that you manage the development of your team in a positive way so that it maximises its performance as a team as quickly as possible.

So just how do you go about recognising how well developed your team is?

Four stages of team development

It's likely your team fits the profile of one of the four stages of development, first seen in the work of BW Tuckman. These are known as:

1 Forming

2 Storming

3 Norming

4 Performing

Each stage has recognisable characteristics and you can generally tell when your team is moving from one stage to the next. These changes can cause problems if you don't recognise and control them. Equally you can use the transition period productively – if you know the signs to look for.

Forming

This is the earliest stage – before people actually see themselves as a team. People tend to feel anxious and cautious and will readily accept your authority as a leader. They are keen to find out what is expected of them as well as the boundaries within which they can act. They will be more concerned with membership issues than about what they need to achieve. They may also compare your team with other teams that they have been part of – and the comparison will probably not be in your favour.

It's important that you make every effort to give the new team members a sense of team identity and help people to define their objectives – both team and individual. If you don't work hard to get people through this phase, it can last a very long time.

Storming

As people understand their role and purpose they become more confident and begin to see themselves as a team, sorting out how they will work together. As they begin to see themselves as a team they may start to exert their right to contribute. They might begin to question what they are doing – and may even begin to question your authority at this stage. On the whole, they'll still look to you for guidance and support. However, conflicts can begin to emerge and sub-groups start to form. This can be based on friendships or, more likely, on common roles and interests.

If you can begin to pass some of the ownership of the various tasks over to the group at this stage, it will help them feel more responsible and confident about what they're doing.

Norming

Once minor conflicts are resolved in terms of who they are and what they are doing, the norming stage is one of co-operation and support. People feel sure about their team identity and the role they are supposed to fulfil. Their level of commitment is increasing – to the task, to you and to one another. Group norms begin to emerge and there's a sense of 'this is the way we do things round here'. The team almost takes on a cultural identity of its own. Team members willingly take on more responsibility for plans and implementation issues.

Your role is really to facilitate this process as you need to use less direct intervention. However, they may still come across issues they feel uncertain about and you will have to intervene to sort these out.

Performing

At this stage of maturity, the team has fully committed to achieving its goals and will take full responsibility for doing so. Team members are prepared to work largely unaided with most responsibility being in their hands. Creativity can thrive as everyone has high self-esteem, there is less conflict and high levels of co-operation develop, both within their own small work group and within the team as a whole.

At this stage your role will probably be working within the group – rather than outside. You will be regarded as a valued colleague rather than as the boss.

The dorming stage

The performing team is naturally what all managers are trying to achieve. However, the management writer John Adair, in his book *Effective Teambuilding* (1987), has identified a further stage that can come after Performing. He refers to this as 'dorming'.

This is a stage of complacency, where people prefer to live on past glories, rather than strive to achieve more. The symptoms are that the team sets up boundaries around itself and has little regard for the needs of others. The team can become ruled by systems and procedures, with things always having to go through the proper channels. The team's results are likely to take a downturn and you can, once again, be isolated from the group. In many cases a thorough restructure is needed and, in the most extreme case, the team may even be disbanded.

The building blocks to an effective team

As leader your job is to get the team to the performing stage as quickly as possible – and keep it there. You need to recognise at which stage of development the team is functioning first of all, before planning how to move the team on.

In the early stages you need to make standards and expectations clear. Team members will need to know the limits of their authority and their main responsibilities. You need to make sure everyone understands their role in context – that is, what they are contributing to the bigger picture. Throughout, people will need to feel valued, with you providing praise and encouragement.

Your team members must also be allowed to make mistakes. These mistakes do not go unnoticed, but people are not punished for them. Instead, they should be viewed as a learning opportunity. You want to encourage creativity, not hinder it. Therefore regular constructive feedback is essential.

The following questions will help you decide at which stage of development your team is – and then adopt strategies to help it move on. Make a mental note of how you respond to each question – the answer will either be you or the team. If most of your answers centre on you as the leader, then the team is probably at the forming or storming stage. If most of your answers centre around the team, then it is on the way to performing.

- Who sets the team direction?
- Who establishes team objectives?
- Who co-ordinates most of the work?
- Who provides most of the creative ideas?
- Who takes on most of the decision making?
- Who acts as arbitrator in situations of conflict?
- Who provides praise and thanks?
- Who provides constructive criticism?
- Who takes responsibility for controlling and monitoring work?
- Who reviews and evaluates the success or otherwise of a project?
- Who provides encouragement and support?
- Who provides training and coaching?
- Who confronts difficult issues and resolves them in an open way?
- Who takes on responsibility for communication?

Positive sign; future challenges

The first sign that teams are working well together is usually the atmosphere surrounding the team. A team working well together is characterised by energy, fun, spontaneity and high productivity. Another sign is that the team builds in plenty of time to review how they work together. They don't just meet when there is a crisis but continually consider how to improve their information systems and relationships. Conflicts are not shied away from but are able to be discussed and resolved rather than buried.

If organisations have found it difficult to build effective teams when team members sit in the same office every day, think of the challenge of building a team when the members are all over the country/world – communicating mainly through computers. With the increase of teleworking and hot desking, new communication challenges are facing organisations. As teams become more remote it will be even more important to build relationships, address isolation issues and tap creativity. What a challenge!

Source: *The Industrial Society* (1998)

Getting there quicker

Clearly, if you are working with a mature team that is performing well, it makes everyone's life easier – especially yours. If this is not the case, what influence can you bring to bear on your team? What can you do to bring them up to speed quickly?

Having a clear focus

One of the main features of a successful team is that its members have a clear focus. This gives them their shared purpose – something they can all strive to achieve. It's almost a vision of where they could be as a team.

It is your role to establish that focus by giving your team the direction it needs in terms of its overall purpose. It answers the question: 'Why are we all here?' Everyone needs to understand the team's reason for being, so you must describe the purpose in relation to the organisation's mission and business objectives.

Your starting point comes from knowing what stage of development your team is currently at. Is it a newly formed team that has little experience of working together, or is it a team nearing maturity?

Understanding its present stage of development will help you work together to mature more quickly, as will having the organisational team processes in place to enable this to happen.

You need to make sure that, not only is the team clear about its purpose, but that everyone else in the organisation is too. Is this how your team would be described in other parts of the organisation?

Once this is established, it's easier for you to take the process to the next stage and set specific team objectives. This should not be done alone. It's important to build commitment by involving the team. They're more likely to take ownership of something they've contributed to. However, in most cases, you will be the one who has final sanction over what those objectives are. It is you who will also have to communicate these to the rest of the organisation and gain its support.

Taking the vision thing too far – a lesson from the top
The problem with creating – and living – powerful, persuasive visions is that they must carry people with them. In recent years, there have been a number of well-documented cases where top managers have lost their jobs following a failure to convince others of the merit of their visions. Their visions of the future were ambitious, credible and possibly achievable, but it did not seem so to their colleagues and subordinates. Instead, all their colleagues could see was a long line of obstacles and impediments to achieving the distant goal. The disenchantment of their people eventually lost the chief executives their jobs. Without followers they became merely men with hats.

Source: *Crainer* (1996)

Acting as ambassador

Acting as ambassador for your team is about developing their reputation within the organisation – with you as their spokesperson. This is particularly important in the early days of a team. No team acts in a vacuum. Organisations just don't function like that. Your team has a clear role, but there is an organisational fit. And increasingly today, one team is dependent on another to allow it to function properly. What you are aiming for is a chain of quality – and your team will be one essential link in that chain.

If the chain breaks down at any point it will have a knock-on effect on other teams – and one of them could be yours. This sort of pressure does nothing to help team development – deadlines are missed, stresses build and timescales become impossible.

Therefore, your role as leader is to build relations with other groups for the good of the team.

You must communicate effectively with other parts of the organisation – if not, your team will be working in isolation. You must be a positive role model, because as your team matures, it is the team who will take over communication. It's all too easy for a team to be inward looking and develop an 'us and them' mentality. You must have seen it yourself – where one department blames another for all its problems, without understanding any of the pressures the other team is under.

However difficult this is (and sometimes it's extremely difficult) it's important not to make negative statements about the efficiency of other teams. Stay positive and work hard to act as an ambassador for your team – particularly with those departments you all depend on to get the job done.

Review and evaluate regularly

To bring a team to maturity means you have to review and evaluate its performance regularly. Not just on a team basis, but on an individual level as well.

You may find that evaluating overall team performance is the easier of the two. It's quite straightforward, for example, to look at the team's objective and measure the result. Of course this assumes that the objective is measurable, so you can actually assess whether it's been achieved or not. The most common format for evaluating an objective is to use the SMART formula, as shown below.

Measurable objectives

Specific –	states exactly what is to be achieved
Measurable –	has a clear measure or outcome
Achievable –	the team has the talent and resources to achieve it
Relevant –	it can be related to the context of the team's overall purpose
Time-related –	it states when the objective should be achieved

Evaluating the success of the team can be easier for you as it is less personal. You are discussing the outcome as a group and personality is less likely to enter into it.

This is not the case with individual evaluation. In this case you need to take care that the feedback discussion you have with individuals is not just a learning exercise, but also focuses on the performance – not the person.

Making individual evaluation meaningful

People need specific job-related feedback to help them grow as individuals and help the team develop. It's an essential role of management. If you don't reinforce good behaviour and try to change poor behaviour people will carry on regardless. It's not that they don't want to change; it's just they don't know that they could. And on a one-to-one basis things can get quite emotional if you don't handle it correctly.

The important point to bear in mind is that feedback must be based on facts. This is the one thing that stops the other person becoming angry or resentful or feeling they have to justify what they did. You must also be clear about your intention in giving feedback. Is it to motivate, i.e. praise something they have done well? Is it to develop i.e. offer constructive criticism of something that has gone wrong? There is a difference in the way these messages are delivered.

There's probably more criticism than praise in organisations today. This may be because it's easier to notice people doing things wrong than doing things right.

However, as the leader of a team, you must look for a balance. If your team is at an early stage of development, it's possible you have more to say on the developmental than the motivational side. Even so, aim for a balance, perhaps starting and finishing with the positives. This way you can get the improvement you are aiming for, while still retaining a good working relationship – and both your self-esteem and that of your team will remain intact. Without effective feedback individuals won't learn and the team won't develop as quickly as it should.

> **Giving motivational feedback:**
> - Select the moment carefully
> - Use positive body language to reinforce what you are saying
> - Focus on an observed behaviour as an example
> - Give a reason why their performance deserves to be praised
> - If possible, say who else recognises their achievement
> - Express genuine feelings of appreciation
> - Avoid going on at length – it avoids embarrassment on both sides.
>
> **Giving developmental feedback:**
> - Make sure others are not listening
> - Have all the facts about what happened – never base criticism on hearsay or opinion
> - Never skirt the issue – come straight to the point
> - Make sure your body language reflects the nature of the issue, without overpowering the other person

- ◆ Aim to address the problem rather than criticise the person
- ◆ Focus on the actions that will put things right/that will improve performance next time – allowing the other person to contribute their ideas
- ◆ Explain what competent performance in this area is like
- ◆ Give your advice if the person has real problems working out the solution for themselves.

Activity 12
Speeding up team development

Objective

Use this activity to plan how to encourage your team to move through the stages of team development.

Task

Identify the current stage of development of your team in terms of forming, storming, norming and performing. Give some examples to support the stage you have identified.

Stage	Evidence

Now list up to four actions that would help the team to move on to the next stage.

The following proforma should help you.

Action	Anticipated outcome	Who is responsible?	End date	Key milestones
1				
2				
3				
4				

Feedback

The actions that you have listed will depend on your team's current stage of development. However, your actions will probably be based around the following themes.

Forming

◆ working with people to define their objectives

◆ helping the team develop a sense of identity

◆ providing praise for even the smallest improvement.

Storming

◆ passing some responsibility for decision making and problem solving to the team

◆ involving team members to a greater extent in reviewing and evaluating the success, or otherwise, of their work

◆ looking at ways to improve communication within the team and with other teams they work with – either internal or external.

Norming

- involving the team in establishing its own objectives
- requiring the team as a whole to resolve conflict rather than deferring to you
- getting the team to co-ordinate its own work
- developing creative thinking within the team, for example, through meetings and brainstorming.

Performing

- passing over your responsibility for controlling and monitoring work
- encouraging team members to train and coach one another
- ensuring the team sets, monitors and evaluates its own objectives.

Who's in my team?

Your team is made up of people with diverse personalities and abilities. Each one has a different and important contribution to make. From your point of view, it's important to understand the various roles people adopt. This way you can help the team to develop further and faster.

Team roles

You probably enjoy some of your work activities and hate doing others. You may like meeting with people and taking on new challenges. You may hate facing unknown situations or the amount of administration in the job. It's just the same for people on the team.

There will be some who enjoy taking the lead, while others prefer to stay in the background. Some may be particularly creative, while others prefer routine, regular tasks. This is a healthy situation, as you need a good mix of people to help the team to function. For example, it's good to be surrounded by creative people – but if the whole team is like that, then nothing would ever get done. People would be so busy creating that no one would actually be doing.

Of course, you have a team in place and so must work with the material you've got. You can't start firing people and bringing new people into the team just because the blend isn't right.

What you can do, however, is to look at parts of the job that aren't done so well and then look at the individuals on your team. This will help you determine if a few abilities are lacking. If so, people can be trained in the necessary skills to give your team a better blend.

Team types

The most famous writer in this field is Meredith Belbin. In his book *The Coming Shape of Organisations* (1996), he argues that a team needs a complementary blend of people to make it work effectively. For example, if you have a team of very intelligent people, expert in their field, the team will not function. There's likely to be a lot of conflict and little empathy. On the other hand, a team of practical and tolerant people could organise themselves but would lack innovation and flexibility.

Table 4.1 shows the team types that he identified, the roles they adopt and key personal characteristics. It also gives their positive qualities and 'allowable weakness'.

You can probably recognise most of these characteristics among your team. You may see different types in the same person. This is not surprising. For example, a completer-finisher may also be a strong teamworker, while a plant may also be a shaper. Some people also have the ability to adopt different types in different situations. This is particularly useful for an effective team.

Belbin also has something to say about management of different teams:

- ◆ **Operational teams** – he believes they can be managed in a semi-hierarchical style, therefore a suitable leader might be a shaper, implementer or completer-finisher

- ◆ **Cross-functional teams** – they involve managing across functions where people are given equal standing, therefore it is better for the leader to be a co-ordinator, teamworker or resource investigator

- ◆ **Strategic teams** – high-level thinking and agreement are essential so the leader could be a monitor-evaluator, co-ordinator or plant.

Team type	Positive qualities	Allowable weaknesses
Implementer 'I turn ideas into action and see they are carried out.' Conservative, dutiful and practical	Organisation skills Common-sense approach Hard-working Self-disciplined	Lacks flexibility Unresponsive to unproven ideas
Co-ordinator 'I get the team to work together to produce results.' Calm, controlled and self-confident	Has a strong sense of objectives Makes use of people's strengths Maximises resources Welcomes all contributors	Can be seen as manipulative Lacks creative ability
Shaper 'I challenge the team's ideas to get results.' Outgoing, dynamic and energetic	Driven to make the team work Challenges inertia Will not tolerate inefficiency and complacency	Can provoke others Prone to impatience
Plant 'I suggest new ideas and strategies to solve problems.' Unorthodox, serious and individualistic	Has a strong intellect and imagination Is knowledgeable Solves difficult problems	Inclined to disregard practical ideas Ignores detail
Resource investigator 'I develop new contacts and initiate projects.' Extrovert, curious and enthusiastic	Capacity for exploring anything new Responds well to challenges	Can lose interest quickly Unlikely to see a project through to the end
Monitor-evaluator 'I evaluate team ideas and analyse problems.' Sober, prudent and unemotional	Uses judgement well Applies discretion Sticks with something and sees it through	Lacks inspiration Cannot motivate others
Teamworker 'I foster a team spirit by supporting other team members.' Sensible, sociable and mild	Responds to different people and situations Promotes a team spirit	Indecisive in moments of crisis Can be easily influenced
Completer-finisher 'I take care of detail and make sure timescales are maintained.' Painstaking, orderly and conscientious	A capacity for follow-through Can be a perfectionist	A reluctance to 'let go' of the control of activities Inclined to worry unduly
Specialist 'I provide key knowledge and skills.' Single-minded, self-starting and dedicated	Provides knowledge that is in rare supply Is skilled in specialist areas	Dwells on technicalities Cannot see the bigger picture – a narrow focus

Table 4.1 *Team types*   Source: *Adapted from Belbin* (1996)

Does it really matter?

The answer to that question is another question. Is your team functioning well as it is? If the answer is 'yes', then it probably doesn't matter. On the other hand, if there do seem to be some gaps in their ability to initiate, undertake and complete a particular project or piece of work, then you might try to do something about it.

You could:

- ◆ choose one particular project that involved all the team
- ◆ look at what went wrong to find out where the problems lie
- ◆ talk to the team about aspects of this work they found difficult – ask them where they can identify the gaps
- ◆ talk to other managers who may be familiar with your team
- ◆ look at the most recent appraisal documentation to see if that gives any hints about missing abilities
- ◆ consider who might be best suited to develop those missing abilities
- ◆ discuss the possibility of training and development with the individuals concerned.

While developing team strengths is vital in your role as a line manager, it's also important not to slavishly follow any one model.

Problems with the Belbin approach include its subjectivity (there is little empirical evidence concerning the personal characteristics of members of highly successful teams) and the difficulty of appraising team as opposed to individual performance. There is little hard evidence that any one mix of team types is any more effective than others.

Source: *Bennett* (1997)

However, if nothing else, Belbin's work provides a useful framework to enable your team to understand its strengths and weaknesses – and do something to redress its weaknesses.

◆ Recap

Identify the stages of team development

- ◆ Tuckman describes the four stages of team development as forming, storming, norming and performing. Managers need to develop their teams to the performing stage as quickly as possible.
- ◆ Adair (1987) warns of a fifth stage, dorming, when a performing team becomes complacent and performance dips.

Explore strategies for developing your team towards peak performance

◆ Strategies that support team development include:

– having a clear purpose or focus that everyone buys into

– acting as ambassador for your team

– regularly evaluating performance and giving motivational and developmental feedback.

Review the mix of skills and attributes required to create a fully effective team

◆ Belbin (1996) advocates that the strongest teams have a diversity of characters and personality types who between them can cover the whole range of team roles.

◆ He describes a team role as 'a tendency to behave, contribute and interrelate with others in a particular way.' There are three action-oriented roles – shaper, implementer and completer-finisher; three people oriented roles – co-ordinator, teamworker and resource investigator; and three cerebral roles – plant, monitor-evaluator and specialist.

 **More @**

Belbin, R. M. (2003) 2nd edition, *Management Teams – Why they succeed or fail*, Butterworth-Heinemann
The acknowledged work on team role theory. See also his website at www.belbin.com

Adair, J. (1987) *Effective Teambuilding: How to Make a Winning Team*, Pan
Explore Adair's model of action-centred leadership.

Try also the websites the **Chartered Management Institute**, www.managers.org.uk, and the **Chartered Institute of Personnel and Development**, www.cipd.co.uk

5 Strengthening the team

Earlier in this book you looked at how the trend towards flattening out hierarchical structures has resulted in greater levels of responsibility being devolved to operational teams.

Giving ownership and responsibility for the work to your team not only helps to achieve your objectives faster, but will also prove motivating for your team. Similarly decisions made by the team are likely to inspire greater commitment to what has been agreed. There are longer-term benefits as well: individuals in the team develop a greater mix of skills and abilities and the potential and flexibility of the team as a whole is strengthened.

Despite the strong case for sharing ownership, many managers still find it remarkably difficult.

> **An empowered team is able to make a difference in the attainment of individual, team, and organizational goals, because it has clear direction and the knowledge, skills, information, and resources to do its job."**
>
> **Mohrman, Cohen and Mohrman 1995**

True delegation, effective delegation is delegation with trust and with only minimum levels of control.

Source: *Handy* (1993)

This theme explores the issues. It introduces the concept of empowerment and explores how you can improve motivation and commitment by delegating responsibility and involving your team in decisions. Finally it considers how you can spread and embed learning throughout your team.

In this theme you will:

◆ **Explore how to empower the people in your team**

◆ **Review the benefits of, and processes for, team decision making**

◆ **Condider how you can promote team learning.**

The power of empowerment

In today's workplace teams are expected to take on more and more responsibility for their own work. You'll find that you spend less time directing and controlling what they do and more time supporting and sustaining their efforts. This change is deliberate – it doesn't happen by accident. And this move towards empowering staff is common in some of the most successful and responsive organisations today.

The concept of empowerment

Empowerment is about you devolving power to members of your team to allow them a higher degree of self-management. You are giving the team ownership for the successful delivery of the end product or service.

Examples of empowerment at work

- The team sets its own work schedules, including work breaks
- The team trains its new members and is involved in selecting recruits
- The team monitors its own work quality and logs quality indicators
- The team solves problems and initiates improvements
- Team members have the authority and discretion to solve customer problems themselves, without having to defer to their boss
- Team members understand what the organisation is trying to achieve and how they are contributing to its goals
- Team members are prepared to ask for resources.

In theory empowerment is a positive concept, but it needs to be introduced and applied well. Telling people they are empowered without setting up systems to support and reward them may well backfire. This is because empowerment is sometimes used as a means of loading more responsibility onto people without giving any reward in return.

Empowerment helps team members make the link between what they do and what the organisation is trying to achieve. It can be extremely motivational because people can see that they make a difference. The team is carrying out its work in the way it sees fit. This can make team members more willing to take risks in an attempt to find a better way of doing things. They're prepared to do this for two reasons – first to improve their own performance and, secondly, they feel they have your permission to make mistakes, so don't have to cover their backs all the time.

But why is empowerment such a popular concept?

And why now?

There are a number of reasons for this. There's a general recognition that many people thrive on challenge. If you give people responsibility, most will welcome it with open arms. In some cases it's a more important part of the job than the salary – although not in all cases. Organisations are realising the truth of the statement people are our greatest asset. This is because people can be creative and innovative, will make suggestions and do improve their way of working – if only they're given the chance.

The other important reason for the change is that you, as a leader, can't do it all. Teams these days have a wide spread of expertise, may be dispersed all over the place and may be involved in a multitude of projects at any one time. You can't control them all; nor should you try. Better to let people get on with things, referring to you for advice and support as required.

However people need permission to do all this. Experience has probably taught them that if they do what they're told, stick to the old ways and don't pass an opinion or comment, it's a good way to stay out of trouble and keep one's self-esteem in tact. Hence the need for empowerment; hence the need for permission that it's okay to:

◆ question the way things have always been done

◆ try new ways of doing things

◆ take responsibility and take risks

◆ make mistakes if the end result is better because of it.

Key features in empowering others

Empowerment is to do with handing over power, while on a practical level, it's making sure the processes are in place to let this happen.

Handing over power is not as simple as it sounds. Some managers are reluctant to do this, usually because they see their power as part of their position. The difference with empowerment is that it's personal power you are using – not power based on the job title.

You may have problems in that some people don't want to take on that power. This may be because it's new to them or it may be that they just don't want the responsibility that goes with empowerment. In fact you can't force someone to be empowered. It's not something you can give. What you can do is enable the other person to be empowered, and we'll look at ways of doing this later in this section.

At the outset, you need to make sure individual, team and organisational objectives are consistent with one another. As the old saying goes: 'If you don't know where you're going, how will you know when you've arrived?' If people are left to their own devices, to get on with things in the manner they see fit, they've got to know exactly where they're heading. This is really an organisational issue, something that needs to be built into the culture.

> A co-operative shoal-of-fish model is desirable, in which each worker is subject to minimal constraints but recognises the security and sustenance benefits of swimming in the general direction of the rest.

Source: *Prof. Sir Frederick Crawford quoted by Crainer* (1996)

If empowerment is going to work, you need to approach it slowly – it won't, and shouldn't, happen overnight. You'll need to explain and train people in what it means and you'll have to make sure the systems are in place to support it. For example, people need to know what they are responsible for and who they are accountable to.

Also, don't assume that everyone has the same capacity to take on responsibility. Some will jump at the chance, others may be reluctant, so you'll have to recognise this in each member of your team. The best way is to start slowly, with delegation.

Delegation – the first step

Handing over power is, at the first level, to do with delegation. If you're a good delegator, you're a long way down the road to empowering others. Delegating is not about dumping jobs you don't want to do on others. It's about handing over real power and authority.

It means:

- ◆ handing over work that is challenging and stretching
- ◆ handing over work to people who might be better than you – without feeling fearful or threatened
- ◆ being fair in the way work is distributed
- ◆ giving other people the chance to develop and coaching them in what to do
- ◆ not worrying and checking up on people all the time
- ◆ taking time to delegate properly – particularly in the early days
- ◆ seeing yourself as a resource not a regulator; a coach not a controller; a support not a supervisor.

You can empower through a mixture of delegation and coaching, helping everyone contribute to team goals. Delegation is only the first stage; empowerment goes further than that. It's also about removing those constraints that prevent someone from being as effective as possible.

The following list shows you what else the delegating manager has to achieve to really empower others.

What does the empowering leader do?

◆ emphasises learning rather than authority and control

◆ enhances and constantly develops the self-esteem of employees

◆ questions and listens

◆ builds relationships throughout the organisation

◆ recognises and acknowledges the role of others

◆ constantly develops others

◆ admits errors

◆ encourages innovation and individual initiative

◆ develops a flexible vision of the future

◆ communicates constantly

◆ coaches and counsels

◆ trusts

◆ abides by high ethical standards.

Source: *Crainer* (1996)

In an empowered organisation people really know what is going on – and have a say in what should happen in the future. The empowered employee not only understands management decisions, but is also given the chance to participate in the decision-making process – sometimes even at policy level. Empowerment can mean an involvement in high-level decision making, an emphasis on sharing ideas and a high level of autonomy for individuals. This kind of input is highly valued by many workers.

While true empowerment may seem a long way down the road from where you are now, there are certain actions you can take to empower your team.

Gaining commitment

Once you can delegate, you're on the way to empowering others. Once that becomes a feature of teamlife, you should be able to set an end-point for a project and let the team decide the how, what and when. In other words, set its own parameters.

From your point of view you must then keep people informed and be available to support them. Communication is key. This doesn't mean you give them the answer every time there's a problem, but you coach them towards their own conclusions. This way, people get used to making decisions for themselves – and are provided with reassurance at a time when they may be feeling vulnerable.

You also need to make sure people know that there is no threat of discipline. People won't be punished for making mistakes – they are simply part of the learning process. This can be difficult for some managers, especially when mistakes happen, as surely they will.

You'll also have to be willing to train people, particularly in each other's jobs. Multi-skilling is a key feature of empowerment but this is where it can fail. It's expensive – both in time and money – but is essential. People need training; they also need resources. You need to make sure the team has everything they need to help them perform. If the organisation is unwilling or unable to provide either of these, any move towards empowerment could fall at the first hurdle.

You also need to be prepared for healthy conflict and debate – and not take this as personal or subversive. It's actually a positive sign that the team is feeling empowered. As a manager you need to reinforce this with rewards for positive behaviour – both on an individual and a team basis. You may not be able to increase salaries, but there are other rewards that team members will find of value. You'd be amazed at how welcome a simple thank you is – and how rarely it's given.

> **Empowerment – responding to customer needs flexibly**
> Federal Express is the first service organisation to win the Malcolm Baldridge National Quality award. The company's motto is 'People, service and profits'. Behind its blue, white and red planes and uniforms are self-managing work-teams, gain-sharing plans and empowered employees seemingly consumed with providing flexible and creative services to customers with varying needs.
>
> At UPS, referred to as Big Brown by its employees, the philosophy was stated by founder Jim Case as: 'Best service at low rates'. Here too we find turned-on people and profits. But we do not find empowerment. Instead we find controls, rules, a detailed union contract, and carefully studied work methods. Nor do we find a promise to do all things for all customers, such as handling off-schedule pick-ups and packages that don't fit size and weight limitations. In fact, rigid operational guidelines help guarantee the customer reliable low-cost service.

Source: *Clutterbuck* (1994)

What the extract seems to highlight is that while an organisation can provide a high standard of service through control and direction, if it wants to move beyond that base towards flexibility and creativity, some form of real empowerment must be in place.

Activity 13
Empowering the team

Objectives

Use this activity to:

◆ find out your team's views on empowerment and how they believe they could feel more empowered

◆ identify ways of improving empowerment.

Task

Hold a team meeting to discuss the issue of empowerment. The following steps will provide a useful structure. Make notes (on a separate sheet of paper) on each step.

1 Ask what the team think the term empowerment means.

2 Agree a definition and note this on a flip chart. Note whether empowerment is seen in a wholly positive light.

3 Ask for their views on how empowered they feel – what do they do in their everyday work that shows they are empowered?

4 Find out what else they need to make them feel more empowered.

5 Consider why this would be good for the team and the business, and state the benefits.

6 Agree the changes that you can make, and what action will be taken; explain the changes you can't make and, if necessary, plan to discuss these with your own manager.

Feedback

There are many definitions of empowerment, but whatever you agree, it should be about devolving power to members of your team to allow them a larger degree of self-management in the successful delivery of the end product or service.

How empowered they presently feel and the ways they could feel more empowered will largely depend on individual circumstances. In other words, how much power you have already devolved to them.

The types of issues that are likely to emerge include the following:

◆ being free to question the way things are done – without being seen as negative

- trying new ways of doing things

- taking more responsibility for how the end result is achieved

- taking risks and making mistakes in an attempt to improve processes – without fear of recrimination

- taking on work that is more challenging and stretching

- being allowed to build on strengths while having weaknesses eliminated

- being coached towards performance improvement

- having work fairly distributed or, better still, agreeing themselves how work will be distributed

- not feeling you are looking over their shoulder all the time

- seeing you as a leader and supporter rather than a manager and controller

- working effectively with other teams across the organisation

- developing the skills of others on the team

- having clear and open lines of communication

- having a high level of trust in the leader and each other

- taking responsibility for their own development

- being involved in decision making

- being rewarded for managing and adapting to change.

The benefits are many and varied. One of the key benefits is that empowerment can improve organisational performance. If you give people responsibility, most will welcome it with open arms – as long as they are fully supported in taking that responsibility. People will improve their way of working, if given the chance, and find creative ways of improving how the team performs. This can have a massive impact on organisational results. On an individual level, empowerment can improve skills, co-operation and self-esteem. It can help an individual's career as it provides more career choices. This means people who are working for you do so because they want to – and not because they feel trapped with nowhere else to go.

Finally, the action you take in the light of this meeting is very important. There may be changes you can make immediately. There may be changes that cannot be made because of organisational constraints. If you are unsure, don't make any promises to the team that you can't keep. It is better to consider all the issues and discuss the matter with others before arriving at a decision.

Decision making in teams

There will be certain decisions that you, as a manager, will have to make yourself. However, many decisions can involve the team. This is for two main reasons. First, you get a variety of ideas and opinions as to the best course of action. Second, if the issue is likely to affect the team, if people have been allowed to put their viewpoint forward, you'll gain more commitment to what's agreed.

Barriers to consensus

Making decisions is probably the most crucial part of your job. It's the means by which problems are solved and choices made. Clearly, there are decisions you have to make alone. For example, in a crisis you're unlikely to seek consensus if a decision needs to be taken quickly. However, with the development of teamwork and the trend towards empowerment, you probably find you're involving your team in more and more decisions.

You may already have an effective method for reaching decisions within the team. Or you may find that with the best of intentions something always goes wrong. This results in you having to take all the decisions, or one or two people on the team always dominating the proceedings.

So what are the common causes of poor decision making within teams?

The first thing to examine is yourself and your own management style. For example, if you tend towards being an autocratic manager, it may seem natural to take all the decisions yourself. On the other hand, you may consult a few team members who you trust, before making a decision. At the other end of the scale, you might call a meeting and work together to reach a decision with which the majority agrees.

A common problem is time. Either you find you haven't the time to canvass opinions from others or there just isn't enough time to debate all the issues fully. In either case you may find it easier to make the decision yourself. It's certainly quicker, but probably less effective.

Giving teams time
...we have often witnessed a phenomenon that we have come to describe as the veneer of consultation. A manager will opt for a highly participative decision-making style in a given situation, often giving the impression of having handed over to his/her team altogether. If the team does not look like making rapid progress, the manager's growing impatience will often cause

him/her to interfere and demand an instant decision, with the threat of an imposed decision if it is not forthcoming. The end result is often a poor quality decision because it has been forced, or one to which there is little commitment because the manager has imposed it.

The frustration and impatience of managers who will not wait for consensus-reaching processes to take their natural course can strangle the development of teamworking.

Source: *Chaudhry-Lawton et al.* (1993)

Another common problem is that the team may be unclear about what they have to decide. This is linked to the time issue and can happen if you don't provide enough information for people on which to base a decision. It can also arise if you and the team are unclear as to what types of decisions you can take. For example, can you make decisions about strategy or policy, or do your decision-making powers rest in areas such as making operational decisions that affect only the team?

Another issue, and a common one, is that some members of the team are more forthcoming with their ideas than others. For example, some may be hesitant to state their opinion, while others may be hostile to the whole idea – 'you're the manager, that's what you're paid for'.

A barrier that commonly arises is that, even when you reach consensus and identify the best solution, there are factors that limit your ability to implement it. This may be to do with resources, cost, lack of information at the time you reached the decision or the impact your decision is going to have on other parts of the business. Of all the barriers, this is the most frustrating and the one you can do little, if anything, about.

Adding creativity with control

Decision making, by its very nature, has to be structured. The following stages are useful in providing control over decisions that are made, without stifling creativity.

Identify the issue

Clarify what it is you and the team need to reach a decision about. Make sure it is within the remit of the team to do something about it and that it is of value to them. Explain how the decision will contribute towards the required outcome, i.e. put it in context.

Review where you are and what has been tried

Explain what has happened so far and, if possible, explain why other decisions or ideas have failed. This will help prevent the team from 'reinventing the wheel'.

Generate options

Generate as many options as possible and don't eliminate any at this stage. Use techniques such as brainstorming to generate a quantity of ideas.

Agree the decision

Establish which decisions will be most effective within the constraints of the organisation, for example, policy, timescales and resources.

Plan what has to be done

Clarify all the steps that need to be taken to implement the decisions. Agree responsibilities and timescales, as well as what other help and resources you will need. Try to identify possible obstacles and show how you are going to overcome these as a team.

Implement and follow up

Communicate your decision to everyone who needs to know. Monitor progress regularly and change the plan if necessary. Celebrate successes and look for ways to solve any ongoing difficulties.

The leader's role in open communication

Your role in this process is crucial, particularly if the team is relatively immature or has not been involved in decision making before. Build in plenty of time for sessions such as the one outlined above. Explain clearly what will happen and what everyone's role will be, reassuring people that everyone's contribution is valuable. It may be useful to set some ground-rules as a group. Common ones include:

- ◆ openness
- ◆ honesty
- ◆ confidentiality
- ◆ conflict without criticism.

Write everything on a flipchart so that people can see the process in action. Make sure everyone contributes, without pressurising individuals and encourage good ideas with praise and thanks. Positive encouragement is the way to obtain people's contribution and the more people who contribute, the more effective the final decision is likely to be.

It may take some time to get it right and it may be frustrating at times as decisions are slow to emerge. However, the outcome is well worth the extra effort as the team grows and learning is improved.

> ... decision-making processes are learning processes. Decision-makers do not begin by knowing all they need to know. They learn as they go along. They learn what is thought practicable and what is not, what is permissible and what is not. By trial and error they find out what can be done and adapt their goals to it.
>
> Source: *J G March quoted by Pugh and Hickson* (1989)

Team learning

You probably spend part of your working day helping individuals on your team to learn. They may each have a training and development plan, which lists activities like work shadowing, reading and workshops, that is designed to improve their skills. But how much time do you spend improving how the *team* learns? Probably very little, because most learning takes place at two levels – individual and organisational – with little thought given to the team wedged between the two.

The case for team learning

> Team learning is the process of aligning and developing the capacities of a team to create the results its members truly desire.
>
> **Peter Senge (1990)**

Everyone needs to know how to do their job properly. The business probably spends a good deal of time and money on making sure this is the case. The problem is people come and go. You can spend a lot of money on an individual who then leaves – and takes their learning with them.

The difference with team learning is that at least some of this is left behind. Because everyone has learned the same lessons, the learning is retained within the organisation.

Team learning is not necessarily about how to work better as a team – although it can be. It's more about harnessing individual talent and learning, and passing this on to the team as a whole.

This is particularly important today as work teams are not as stable as they were. Cross-functional teams, virtual teams and global teams make this an even bigger challenge. You could also argue that team learning takes on even greater importance because there can be a more widespread cross-pollination of ideas.

As team leader, your role is key.

> Effective team leaders do two things extremely well. First, they balance the tasks they give to people, so there is constant stretch and just enough nurturing to help people overcome any under or over-confidence they may have. Employees in such an environment feel they are constantly learning more, yet know support is always there... The second thing effective team leaders do well is to facilitate the environment where people feel encouraged to help each other learn and are confident they can do so. In part, this is about clarifying learning roles, but it also involves setting an example in managing their own learning and enabling the team to create what many regard as a luxury – reflective space.

Source: *Clutterbuck* (2000)

Single loop versus double loop learning

Professor Chris Argyris explained the idea of double loop learning in his book, *On Organisational Learning* (1993). Most organisations work at single loop level. This means errors are corrected once they have been made. In other words, applying existing methods and knowledge in terms of 'this is the way things are done round here'. It's very reactive – make a mistake, then put it right. It's also centred on the here and now.

Double loop learning means employees are encouraged to question what they do and continually look for ways of making improvements. It can happen at job level or it can happen at organisational level – questioning the whole basis on which the business is structured, be it policies, systems or processes. This is proactive learning and is looking to the future – not necessarily what is happening in the present. It requires a supportive climate and is actually a feature of an empowered organisation.

Double loop learning will improve team learning. Your team will not just be looking to put things right, but asking why it went wrong in the first place and what they can do to make sure it doesn't happen again. As the manager, this can sometimes be uncomfortable as they are always asking 'why?' On the plus side, it means the team is always looking to learn and improve, which is the end result you should be looking for.

For example, Hewlett-Packard has set up learning communities. These are informal groups of people who come together to discuss best practice, issues or skills. HP's vision of this is 'that our consultants feel and act as if they have the entire organisation at their fingertips'. They have also introduced project snapshots and knowledge-mapping supported by software designed for group communication and shared group use.

Overcoming common barriers

As manager, your role is to facilitate team learning. A major part of this is recognising what barriers are in the way of team learning – and finding ways of overcoming them. Individuals and the team need to commit to, and take ownership of, their own learning – this is the ideal.

Valuing learning

A common problem in many organisations is that learning is under-valued – it's something people can do in their own time. In fact, learning is essential for growth but because you can't actually see it taking place, it's low down the priority list. There's still an inclination for people to want to look busy to justify their job. However, you'll need to take the lead in showing that you value learning. People who never take time to reflect, never learn anything. They just carry on making the same mistakes – and making the same adjustments to put things right. Build in reflection time for the team as a whole to sit down together, discuss what they do and, most importantly, how they can improve. The brave manager will also build in time for people to question why they are doing it.

Of course if you're building in time to learn, attitudes may have to change. It's still a commonly held view that learning is the same as training and all training takes place on a course. Not true. While a course will teach people knowledge and skills to do their job, it won't necessarily help team learning. Team learning comes from experience, discussion and a host of other methods.

Understanding learning styles

It can be extremely helpful if you know how people on your team learn. Everyone has a different learning style, so if you can match activities to those styles, people will learn more effectively. For example, some people learn best by doing, while others prefer to stand back and plan an approach. Others prefer to think about things in depth before arriving at an answer. If you can find ways of accommodating these different styles, you're well on the way to improving team learning. So, you'll have to look at how you can provide as wide a range of learning opportunities as possible. This also adds interest and helps maintain enthusiasm.

Applying learning in practice

Time to apply learning is always an issue. Have you ever undertaken some form of training or development and never used any of it at work? It's common. Sometimes it is because the activity didn't meet your needs. Often it is because there was never any time to think about what you had learned and apply your new skills. So you slip back into the old tried and trusted methods. The same is true of team learning. Unless you give people time to think about and apply their new learning, things will never change.

Structuring learning

Another barrier can be that learning is haphazard. If you want your team to get into the double loop learning outlined above, this cannot be the case. It needs some structure – particularly in the early days. Therefore you'll need to discuss objectives (what the team is trying to achieve/learn overall) and you'll need to measure the outcomes (has the team achieved what it set out to do?). Once this becomes a habit, you may be able to step out of the loop as evaluating learning becomes almost second nature.

Good behaviour must be reinforced. People need to know when they're doing well – so reward is an essential part of learning.

Recognising success to enhance team learning

For some people learning is a reward in itself, but for others this is not the case. If asked, most people would say they feel rewarded by money. However, you may not be in a position to offer this and, in fact, the impact of money may be short-lived. Money can be thought of as a maintenance factor. Everybody needs it, but it doesn't guarantee continued efforts in the right direction. So if you're not in a position to pay people more, there are better ways of rewarding team success.

True rewards come under categories such as the following:

- credit for a job well done, for example praise, encouragement and gratitude
- the work itself, for example the chance to be more creative or undertake favourite work tasks
- greater responsibility, for example new tasks or more challenging projects
- providing scope for further learning, for example more development opportunities
- recognition, for example from senior management or the organisation as a whole through a team award.

The challenging part for you is to decide which is most appropriate, because rewards mean different things to different people. Ask people what matters to them. What would maintain their present efforts to improve team learning? You may be able to reward the team as a whole, but it's just as likely you'll have to reward on an individual basis. This may seem to undermine the concept of team learning. But what you must never lose sight of is the fact that the team is made up of individuals. And individuals can be very different.

The learning organisation

The whole organisation, comprising all its people, must develop in order to:

♦ adapt to threats and changes

♦ pursue opportunities

♦ realise potential.

This requires an appropriate organisational environment and culture which recognises that learning:

♦ requires experience, experiment and exploration

♦ necessitates risk taking

♦ requires openness and challenge

♦ is an on-going 'never completed' process.

To be effective in developing its people an organisation must not only provide training and development but also clearly demonstrate the value of learning.

Source: *Wild* (1994)

Activity 14
Improving team learning

Objective

This activity can help you to consider ways of improving how the team learns.

Case study

Read the following case study.

Training and learning

We separate learning from the environment, the problem and the people involved. We tend to see training and learning as a separate process from implementation – the 'doing'. Learning is not an activity that is carried out in isolation, but is part of the constant flow of adaptation and experimentation, which is done in partnership with others in the organisation, the organisation itself and the environment in which the learner finds him/herself.

Part of the process of learning together is creating the opportunity for practice. For a group to learn together effectively, the starting point has to be the ability to reflect on issues such as assumptions held within the group, successes and failures. If we understand the reasons for our success we could duplicate the strategies. Equally if we understand the reasons for failure, we can do something different.

A key aspect to successful teams is the understanding of the differences within the team and how to value these differences. Harnessing these differences will benefit the individuals and the organisation in the achievement of goals and objectives.

We need diversity to ensure all angles of an issue are being explored. It is in diverse groups that the power of dialogue is a fundamental skill in maximising the potential for learning and creativity [in a way that is] beyond the understanding and knowledge of one individual.

A fundamental result of the process of learning for both the individual and organisation is that through the process of learning we recreate ourselves; we become more of who we are capable of being. For the organisation to expand the possibilities and options of what it could become, learning in all its many facets should feature high on everyone's list of priorities.

Source: *Keene* (1999)

Task

In the light of what you have read, talk to other colleagues – your manager, your peers and team members – and decide how learning can be improved within your own team. Make notes on your ideas.

Learning need	How it can be met	Desired business improvement	Who is involved	End date

Feedback

An initial, important point is to ensure that any structured event can always be linked into the department's objectives and, hence, what the organisation is trying to achieve overall. Also make sure that any event builds in time for discussion, brainstorming and feedback, to make sure everyone has time to contribute their own diverse views. This way the team learns from one another. As a manager, it is also important to ensure people who have attended a training or development event should be allowed time to practise back at work – otherwise new knowledge and skills can be quickly lost if not applied. Also, look beyond conventional training courses as the only way people learn. Consider a range of activities, from reading, open learning or e-learning to secondment, work-shadowing and job swaps.

Learning does not only take place during a formal event. Learning is a continuous process. People learn all the time and they learn best from one another, when faced with difficult decisions or common problems to solve, for instance. Learning in this way can be more effective and is more likely to bring major shifts in the way people think and act. However, people need time to assimilate that learning, so it is important that you enable this to happen, for example, by allowing time for reflection, asking questions and giving feedback. Operationally, this may seem difficult, but it is essential so that people can assimilate what they have learned and improve the way they work – rather than making the same mistakes time and time again.

You could even arrange internal team events to review learning and share best practice among the team. Such events are also useful to help you shift the balance away from you (as representative of the organisation), to them (as a team), to give them the chance to manage their own learning and development. As the article says:

> As employees we have to let go of the comfort of a secure environment and instead, take up the challenges of self-responsibility and self-development. As individuals discover security in their own abilities and employability and learn to balance the paradox of security and uncertainty, their performance increases.

Source: *Keene* (1999)

Activity 15
Action planning to improve teamworking

Objectives

Use this activity to:

◆ summarise your work in this book

◆ develop an action plan to improve teamworking.

This book is about your team and improving the way it works and you lead. It is important to document the actions you are going to put in place to make positive and lasting changes that the whole team supports.

Task

In the light of the activities you have completed so far (Activities 1–14), develop an action plan to improve teamworking. Choose between four and six actions that would help to improve how the team works together. These can be actions around your own leadership or things you require the team to do.

1 Write down the objective for each – what you are trying to achieve.

2 List the task(s) required in order to achieve the objective.

3 Write down any support needed, for example people, resources, time.

4 Make a note of who is responsible for seeing it through.

5 Write in any milestone dates – when stages of the objective might be completed.

6 Put in a realistic end date.

You can set out your action plan in the way that best suits you. An example is given here, together with a blank chart you can complete.

Team action plan

Objective	Tasks	Support	Responsibility	Milestones	End date
To implement a system of monthly feedback meetings with the team to improve our learning within six months	Evaluate value of T&D activity	MJ (monitors T&D activity)	Self	Sept 2004	
	Present to team on concept, purpose & roles	Talk to HR about key themes	Self, maybe HR rep.	Oct 2004	
	Set up meetings	–	Self	Oct 2004	
	Hold three meetings	Team	Self & team	Jan 2005	
	Evaluate				Jan 2005

Team action plan

Objective	Tasks	Support	Responsibility	Milestones	End date

Feedback

Once developed, check your action plan to ensure it is clear what will be achieved and that the timescales are realistic. Discuss it with your own manager for their input.

Remember, it is an action plan to improve teamworking, so show it to others on the team whose support you will need in its implementation. If people are involved in the decision making, they are more likely to commit to seeing it through.

◆ Recap

Explore how to empower the people in your team

◆ Empowerment means devolving power and responsibility to team members to give them a higher degree of self-management. The benefits are greater motivation and improved skill levels and performance.

◆ You can empower through a mix of delegation and coaching but first you need to build a team environment in which empowerment can take place. This involves open communication to build trust, commitment to support individual development and willingness to learn from mistakes.

Review the benefits of, and processes for, team decision making

◆ The benefits of involving your team in decision making are a greater pool of knowledge, different perspectives, greater understanding of the problem and increased acceptance of the solution.

◆ Barriers to team decision making include reluctance of the line manager to let go, time constraints, poor definition of the decision to be made, personality conflicts and reluctance of team members to get involved.

◆ A structured decision-making process provides a framework for improving team decision making.

Consider how you can promote team learning

◆ You can encourage your team to learn by involving them in decision making and encouraging them to learn through experimentation and sharing their learning from past experiences.

◆ Double loop learning occurs when the whole team or organisation learns from an individual. The learning is incorporated into policies, systems and processes and fed through the organisation.

◆ Team leaders should encourage learning behaviour through reward. Options include recognition and praise, an opportunity for more challenging work, greater responsibility and opportunities for further development.

▶▶ **More @**

Blanchard, K., Carlos, J. and Randolph, A. (2001) *3 Keys to Empowerment: Release the Power Within People for Astonishing Results,* **Berrett-Koehler Publishers Inc**
This book explains the concrete steps managers can take to fully empower their employees.

Whitmore, J. (2002) *Coaching For Performance: Growing People, Performance and Purpose,* **Nicholas Brealey Publishing**
This influential work on coaching introduces using the GROW sequence – Goals, Reality, Options, Will – to generate prompt action and peak performance.

Senge, P. (1993) *The Fifth Discipline: The art and practice of the learning organization,* **Random House Business Books**
The author defines five business 'disciplines' which help to build 'learning organizations'.

References

Adair, J. (1987) *Effective Teambuilding: How to Make a Winning Team*, Pan

Adair, J. (1997) *Leadership Skills*, Chartered Institute of Personnel and Development

Agyris, C. (1993) *On Organisational Learning*, Blackwell

Arkin, A. (1999) 'Peak Practice', *People Management*, 11 November, 57-59

Belbin, R. M. (1996) *The Coming Shape of Organisations*, Butterworth-Heinemann

Belbin, R. M. (2003) 2nd edition, *Management Teams – Why they succeed or fail*, Butterworth-Heinemann

Bennett, R. (1997) *Organisational Behaviour*, Pitman Publishing

Bing, J. W. and Mercer Bing, C. (2001) 'Helping Global Teams Compete', *Training and Development*, March, 70

Blake, R. R. and Mouton, J. S. (1985) *The Managerial Grid III*, Gulf Publishing Company

Butcher, D. and Harvey, P. (1999) 'Be Upstanding', *People Management*, 30 June, 39–42

Chaudhry-Lawton, R., Lawton, R., Murphy, K. and Terry, A. (1993) *Quality: change through teamwork*, Century Business

Clutterbuck, D. (2000) 'Time to Focus Learning on the Team', *Training Journal*, April, 12

Covey, S. (1992) *The Seven Habits of Highly Successful People*, Simon & Schuster

Crainer, S. (1996) *Leaders on Leadership*, Institute of Management

Elgin, R. (2001a) 'No more Mr Nice Guy as times get tough', *The Sunday Times*, Appointements section 4 March

Elgin, R. (2001b) 'Shackleton's lesson in leadership', *The Sunday Times*, Appointments section, 4 March

The Grass Roots Group Plc (2003) *Respect for People*, www.grg.com

Handy, C. (1993) *Understanding Organizations*, Penguin Books

Hannagan, T. (1998) *Management Concepts and Practices*, Pitman Publishing

Harvard Davis, S. (2001) 'How to Measure Team Effectiveness: a Model,' *Training Journal*, February, 24–26

Hersey, P. (1984) *The Situational Leader*, Centre for Leadership Studies

Howes, D. (1998) 'Future hinges on global teams', *The Detroit News*, 21 December

The Industrial Society (1996) 'Management Competencies', *Managing Best Practice* series, No. 21

The Industrial Society (1998) 'Teamworking', *Managing Best Practice* series, No. 47

Johnson, P. and Gill, J., (1993) *Management Control and Organisational Behaviour*, Paul Chapman Publishing

Jones, P., Palmer, J., Osterweil, C. and Whitehead, D., (1996) *Delivering Exceptional Performance*, Pitman Publishing

Katzenbach, J. R. and Smith, D. S. (1994) *The wisdom of teams: Creating the High Performance Organisation*, HarperCollins

Keene, A. (1999) Training and learning: a muti-desciplined approach', *Training Journal*, November

Keuning, D. (1998) *Management: A Contemporary Approach*, Pitman Publishing

McGregor, D. (1987) *The Human Side of Enterprise*, Penguin

McLachlan, R. (1998) 'Regeneration X', *People Management*, 2 April

Mohrman, S., Cohen, S. and Mohrman, A. (1995) *Designing Team-Based Organizations*, Jossey-Bass

Mullins, L. (1996) *Management and Organisational Behaviour*, Pitman Publishing

Office for National Statistics, www.statistics.gov.uk

Peters, T. (1987) *Thriving on Chaos*, Pan

Pugh, D. S. and Hickson, D. J. (1989) *Writers on Organisations*, Penguin BooksReynolds, L. (2000) 'What is Leadership?' *Training Journal*, 27

Rushe, D. (2001) 'Wal-Martians', *The Sunday Times* – Business Section, 10 June

Senge, P. (1990) *The Fifth Discipline: The art and practice of the learning organisation*, Doubleday

Spencer, J. and Pruss, A. (1993) *Managing your Team*, Piatkus

Tannenbaum, R. and Schmit, W. H. (1973) 'How to choose a leadership pattern', *Harvard Business Review*, May/June

Wild, R. (1994) 2nd edition, *How to Manage*, BCA

Williams, P. (1997), *The Magic of Teamwork*, Thomas Nelson Publishers

Management Extra

LEADING TEAMS